THE MULTICULTURAL GAME BOOK

More than 70 Traditional Games from 30 Countries

by Louise Orlando

SCHOLASTIC
PROFESSIONAL BOOKS

New York • Toronto • London • Auckland • Sydney

To My Family
Thanks Mom and Dad for all your help

Text and interior design by Ellen Matlach Hassell
for Boultinghouse & Boultinghouse, Inc.

Cover design by Vincent Ceci

Cover illustrations by Teresa Anderko

Interior illustrations by Teresa Anderko, Delana Bettoli,
Ellen Matlach Hassell, and Mona Mark

ISBN 0-590-49409-0

Contents

Introduction

For thousands of years, people have played games to teach or sharpen skills for survival, to bring whole communities together, and for simple enjoyment. Like music, folktales, and holiday traditions, games can teach us a lot about each other. By learning games from other parts of the globe, we learn about new customs, beliefs, and pasts. In addition, we learn a little more about our own society and culture, and the places our families came from.

The Multicultural Game Book provides teachers of grades 1–6 with over 70 fun ways to create and foster an understanding of world cultures.

Used on their own, the games act as an introduction to different cultures. Integrated into the curriculum, they assist teachers in their interdisciplinary planning by helping students build on math, language arts, social studies, art, and physical development. For instance, a lone game of French Solitaire (page 67)

not only builds on students' problem-solving skills, but also teaches students how to appreciate and enjoy themselves when alone.

Replicating game boards employs students' creativity, art and math skills. Language arts skills are used as children read, listen, and follow directions. Students can be encouraged to use their writing skills to write about games, and make up extensions of these games to be played by others. Learning about other countries, their locations, and the period in history when the games were invented, teaches social studies skills.

As children play these games, they not only develop an appreciation for world cultures, they also learn about and reenact the steps taken by children thousands of years ago. This type of authentic instruction helps children step back in time and understand a little more about life in other parts of the world.

The games in this book are appropriate for children between the ages of six and twelve. The rules are simple, can be quickly understood, and picked up with little teacher assistance.

Many games require few supplies, and can be played on a classroom desk, floor, or playground. Only a few games, like *Quilles* (page 69) require extra materials and effort. These games are included to help students understand the important role games played in cultures where strong community spirit and the need for group cooperation were a necessity for survival. Some games can be played alone or in pairs while other games teach the importance of team cooperation for ultimate victory.

Many games in this book have been popular for hundreds of years and continue to be played as we approach the 21st century—where high tech competes with yesterday's games using pebbles and sticks.

Included with each game is its original name, and when available, its translation, brief notes on its origin, and cultural significance. In addition, there are some games which students may already be familiar with, such as *Ampe* (page 16) and *Jan-Kem-Po* (page 49). These were included to help stimulate students' thinking about how ideas and information are shared between different cultures.

Whether or not the games are used on their own or to enhance a particular lesson, I know you and your students will enjoy and learn from them as much as I did.

—*Louise Orlando*

Materials

All these materials can be easily found or inexpensively bought.

Bottle caps (plastic and metal)

Cardboard

Checker pieces

Chess pieces

Coins

Coloring supplies

Construction paper

Deck of cards

Dice

Dried beans

Egg cartons

Glue

Hula-hoops

Jump ropes

Oak tag

Paper dots

Pebbles

Plastic bowls (margarine tubs)

Puzzles

Rulers

Scarf or fabric for blindfolds

Scissors

String

Unpopped popcorn

AFRICA

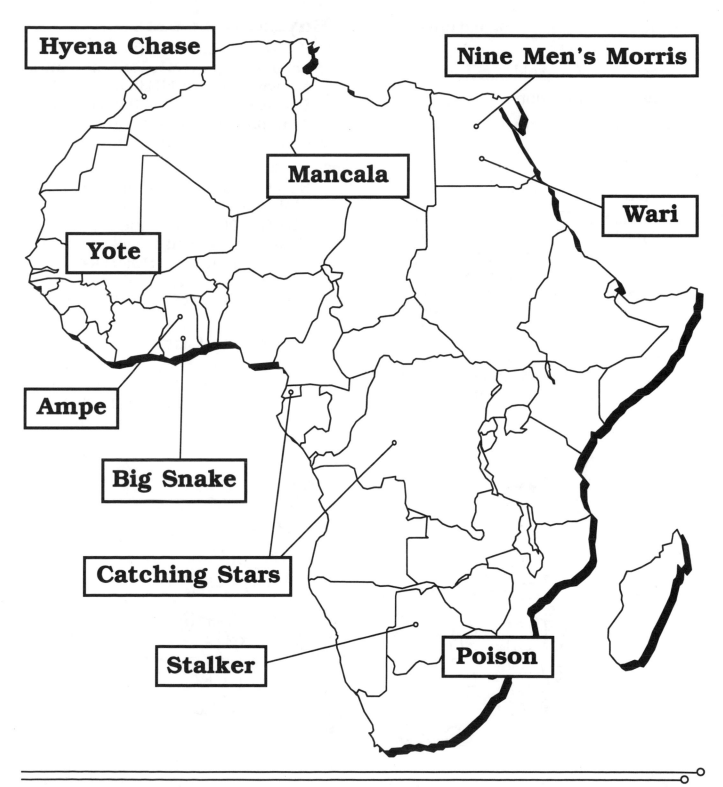

Hyena Chase

Nine Men's Morris

Mancala

Wari

Yote

Ampe

Big Snake

Catching Stars

Stalker

Poison

Stalker

Skills: Large motor and listening skills

Ages: 7 and older

Players: 7 or more

Materials: Two scarves for blindfolds

Watch or timer

About the Game

The *springbok* is an animal similar to a gazelle, but is found only in southern Africa. Like many games from this region, this one is about a real-life skill: hunting. For centuries children have played this game imitating adult Bushmen stalking a springbok.

Through play, children learn the life-long skills of good hunters: patience, concentration, hand-eye coordination.

Playing the Game

1. Have all the players form a circle. Choose two players to start the game: one will be the HUNTER, the other the SPRINGBOK. Blindfold them both and then spin them around. Have one player announce for the hunt to begin.

2. Moving quietly within the circle, the HUNTER tries to catch the SPRINGBOK, while the SPRINGBOK tries to avoid the HUNTER. Players forming the circle can either remain silent or make animal noises to distract the HUNTER and SPRINGBOK. No one is allowed to touch the HUNTER and SPRINGBOK.

Ending the Game

After a set period of time, if the HUNTER fails to catch the SPRINGBOK, the "animal" wins and a new HUNTER is brought out. If the SPRINGBOK is caught, two new players take over.

Nine Men's Morris

Skills: Thinking and planning skills

Ages: 8 and older

Players: 2

Materials: Copy of game board (page 12)

18 playing pieces (9 per person)—two different colors

About the Game

The first reported *Nine Men's Morris'* game board dates back to 1400 B.C. to an ancient Egyptian temple. What makes a game remain popular for so many years? It's easy to play and the game board is simple enough to be drawn on the ground or a piece of paper. During the Bronze Age, the game (like many others throughout the years) was carried to Ireland by traders from Greece or Phoenicia. Making its way across Europe, the game picked up names such as *mérelles*, *mühle* or *mill*.

Playing the Game

1. This is a game of position where the object is to form lines of three in a row and in turn capture your opponent's pieces.

2. To begin, players take turns placing pieces (one at a time) on any of the vacant dots on the board.

3. When all the pieces are on the board, players take turns moving their pieces—one at a time—along a straight line to an adjacent vacant dot.

4. As a player moves, he or she tries to form a *mill*—three pieces in a row. When a mill is formed, the player may capture a piece from his or her opponent that *does not* belong to a mill. The only time a piece from a mill may be taken is if there are no other pieces open.

Winning the Game

A player must take all but two of the opponent's pieces or block his or her opponent from moving.

Nine Men's Morris Game Board

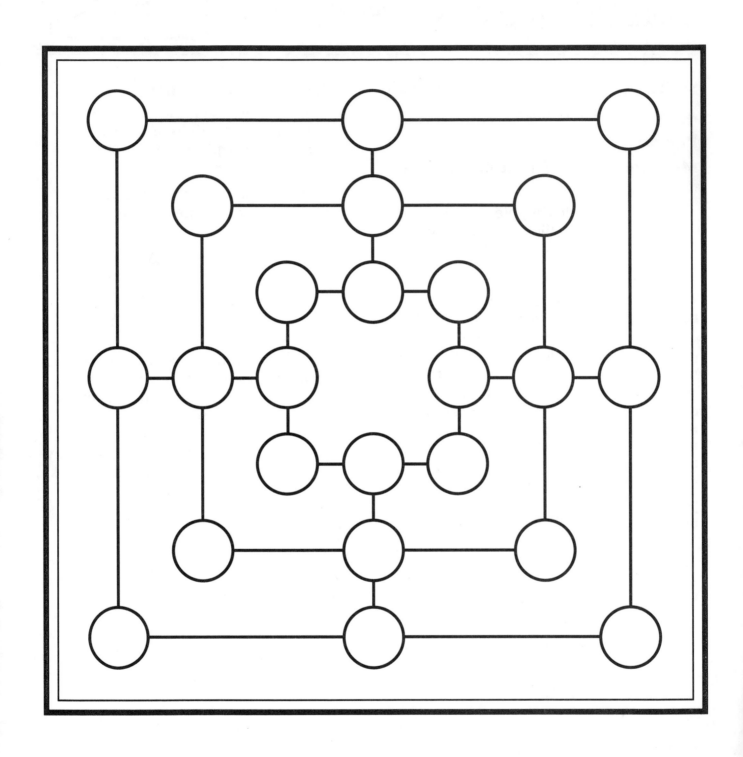

Wari

Skills: Thinking, planning and strategy skills

Ages: 9 and older

Players: 2

Materials: Copy of game board (page 14) or egg carton or 12 small containers, cups, or jar lids

48 playing pieces

About the Game

Wari is thousands of years old. It is a version of *Mancala* (page 20). This thinking game originated in Egypt and is played in many African and Middle Eastern countries, as well. In poorer areas where players couldn't afford Wari boards made of wood or baked clay, they would make their own boards in the soft ground.

A version of Wari, called *Awari*, was brought from Africa to Surinam, in South America, by African slaves. To many, this game holds religious and spiritual significance. The game is played at funerals the day before a body is buried to entertain the body's spirit which has yet to "leave." At sundown, all play stops for fear that the ghosts will join the players and fly away with their spirits.

For spiritual reasons, men whose wives have died are the only ones allowed to make Awari boards. The boards are roughly hacked from logs. This is done on purpose to avoid bad fortune. The boards are smoothed to perfection over time by players' fingers.

Playing the Game

1. Players pick a side and place four playing pieces in each of their six holes (see drawing).

2. Play always moves counterclockwise. Player one begins by taking all the pieces from *any* hole on his or her side and placing one piece in each of the next four spaces. Players take turns repeating this step.

3. During a turn, if the last piece of a move is placed in an opponent's hole that has two or three pieces in it, the player captures all the pieces. He or she also wins the pieces in adjacent holes which contain two or three pieces. Captured pieces are removed from the board.

4. If a hole contains 12 or more pieces, the player must "sow" them to different holes—always skipping over the hole they were taken from.

5. If a player's holes are all empty, and his or her opponent can't fill them, the player wins all the pieces left on the board.

Winning the Game

Capture the most pieces and be the first to empty all your holes.

Wari
Game
Board

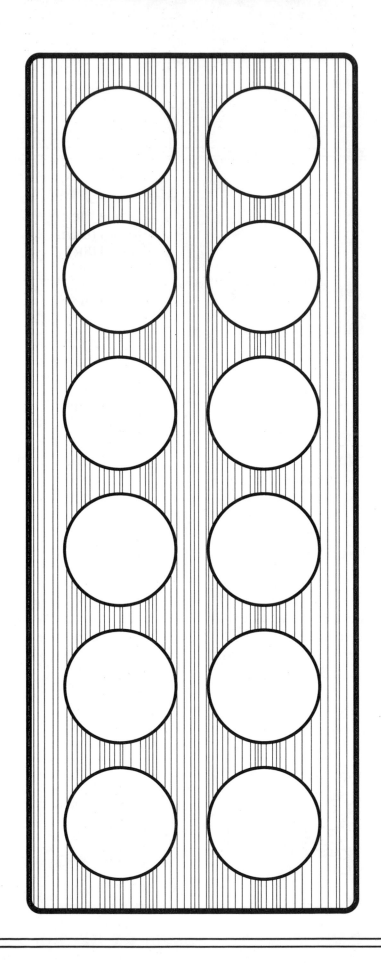

Catching Stars

▶ PLACE OF ORIGIN ◀
Equatorial Guinea, Zaire

Skills: Large motor skills

Ages: 7 and older

Players: 7 or more

Materials: Playground or other large running area

About the Game

Since the beginning of time, people from around the world have been fascinated by stars. What are they? Why are they there? Where did they come from? What stories do they tell? This game is played by children of African Pygmy tribes who have long been intrigued by the night sky.

Playing the Game

1. Divide the players into two groups: STARS (a third of the players) and CATCHERS (remaining players).

2. Set up two parallel boundaries, about 20 feet apart (6 meters).

3. The CATCHERS stand in the middle of the boundaries while the STARS stand on one boundary. The CATCHERS begin the game by reciting together:

   Star light, star bright
   How many stars are out tonight?

   The STARS respond:

   More than you can catch!

   And then make a mad dash to the other boundary—trying not to be tagged by a CATCHER.

4. Tagged STARS become CATCHERS. The game continues with both sides reciting the verse until all STARS are caught.

Winning the Game

Last person to be tagged wins the game!

Ampe

One! Two! Three!

One! Two! Three!

Skills: Quick reactions

Ages: All ages

Players: 2

Materials: None

About the Game

In the United States, children call this game *Odds and Evens.* Using only their hands, players pick "odds or evens." Next, they make a fist and call out "1, 2, 3 Shoot!" and throw out any number of fingers between one and four. The number of fingers showing—odd or even—decides who wins. In southern Ghana and in parts of China this game is played with a slight twist. In Ghana, the game called *Ampe* is a matter of getting the right foot forward, so to speak. While in China, it is called *Challenge*, a guessing game (see page 29).

Playing the Game

1. Two players face each other. One takes EVENS, the other ODDS. Together they clap their hands and shout "One! Two!" and on "Three!" each sticks out a foot.

2. Scoring:

   • If players stick out facing feet (left for one, right for the other), EVENS wins a point.

   • If players stick out opposite feet (the same feet), ODDS wins.

3. Once this is mastered, the game gets harder. On the second clap players jump once before sticking out a foot. The game can continue with players making up movements to do before shooting out their legs.

Winning the Game

The first person to reach 11 is the match winner.

Big Snake

Skills: Quick reflexes, coordination, cooperation and large muscle skills

Ages: 6 and older

Players: 10 or more

Materials: Playground or other large running area

A whistle

About the Game

Ghana's warm climate is home to many types of snakes. Here's a game that calls attention to the cold-blooded reptile. It's similar to the Chinese game of *1, 2, 3 Dragon* (see page 28).

Playing the Game

1. Players pick one person to be the SNAKE. The SNAKE goes to his or her home, an area large enough to fit several people which you may want to mark off with cones.

2. At the sound of a whistle, the SNAKE comes out of its home and tries to tag other players. Tagged children join hands with the SNAKE and try to catch the others.

3. The original SNAKE is always the leader and determines who its "body" will go after. The SNAKE'S head and tail are the only parts that may tag "free players."

4. If the SNAKE'S body "breaks," the SNAKE must return home, regroup, and start again. Free players may try to break the SNAKE, forcing it to return home.

Ending the Game

The game ends once everyone is caught or completely out of breath.

Hyena Chase

Skills: Counting

Ages: 8 and older

Players: 3 or more

Materials: One playing piece per player (pieces should be different colors or shapes)

One playing piece for Hyena (completely different from the others)

Copy of the game board (page 19)

A die

About the Game

People of all ages play this game of chase in the North African country of Morocco. The object of the game is to get your mother from the village (largest circle on board) to the well (middle of the spiral) without her being eaten by a hyena. Each of the smaller circles along the "path" represent days.

At one time, pieces were moved by throwing sticks into the air. Now a die is used as a substitute.

Playing the Game

1. The size of the board—number of days (or circles) from the village to the well—is left to the players and is traditionally drawn on the ground. Playing pieces are called MOTHERS.

2. The first player to roll a six, places his MOTHER on the first "day" (or small circle) and gets to roll and move again.

Note: Any player who rolls a six and is outside the village gets to roll and move again.

3. Two or more MOTHERS may occupy the same "day."

4. MOTHERS can only enter the well with an exact roll. So if a player's MOTHER is two days away from the well, the player must roll a two before moving.

5. At the well, the MOTHER stays, to "wash her clothes," until the player rolls a six, and begins MOTHER'S return to the village.

6. The first person to get MOTHER back to the village wins the HYENA counter and begins the journey back to the well. To leave the village, the HYENA must roll a six. Once out, HYENA moves twice as fast as the MOTHERS. For example, if the player rolls a 2, HYENA moves 4.

7. HYENA can only enter the well with an exact roll and leave it with a roll of six. On the HYENA'S return to the village from the well, the MOTHERS he or she passes are "eaten" and removed from the board.

Winning the Game

Be the first to get the HYENA. The more MOTHERS "eaten," the higher the score.

Hyena Chase Game Board

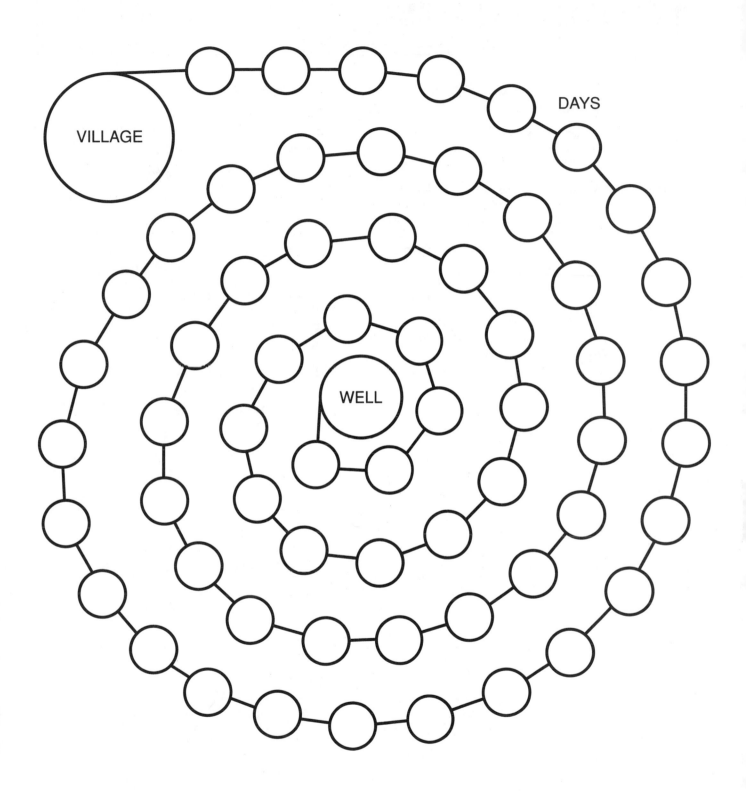

Mancala

Skills: Thinking, planning and strategy skills

Ages: 9 and older

Players: 2

Materials: Copy of game board (page 21) or egg carton plus two small containers or 14 small containers, cups, or jar lids

36 playing pieces

About the Game

Mancala is the name given to a number of strategy games which have been played in Africa and Asia. These games are believed to be some of the oldest board games around. This version of Mancala is called *Kalaha* and is over 7,000 years old. Boards were found in the Amon Temple in Karnak, Egypt. Carved boards were also found along caravan routes.

Playing the Game

1. Players pick a side and place three playing pieces in each of their six holes. The holes at either end are common property called *Kalaha*.

2. Play always move counterclockwise. Player one begins by taking all the pieces from *any* hole on his or her side and placing one piece in each of the next three spaces—including, if necessary, the Kalaha at the end. The player may also place his or her pieces in the holes on his or her opponent's side.

   If a player's last piece lands in his or her Kalaha, that player takes another turn. Players take turns repeating this step.

3. If a player lands on an empty space on their opponent's side, he or she can take the pieces from the hole directly across from the one he or she just landed in and place them in the empty space. If there are no pieces in the hole, his or her turn is over.

4. The game ends when all the holes on one side of the board are empty. The player with pieces left in his or her holes, puts them in his or her Kalaha.

Winning the Game

The player with the most pieces in his or her Kalaha wins the game.

Mancala Game Board

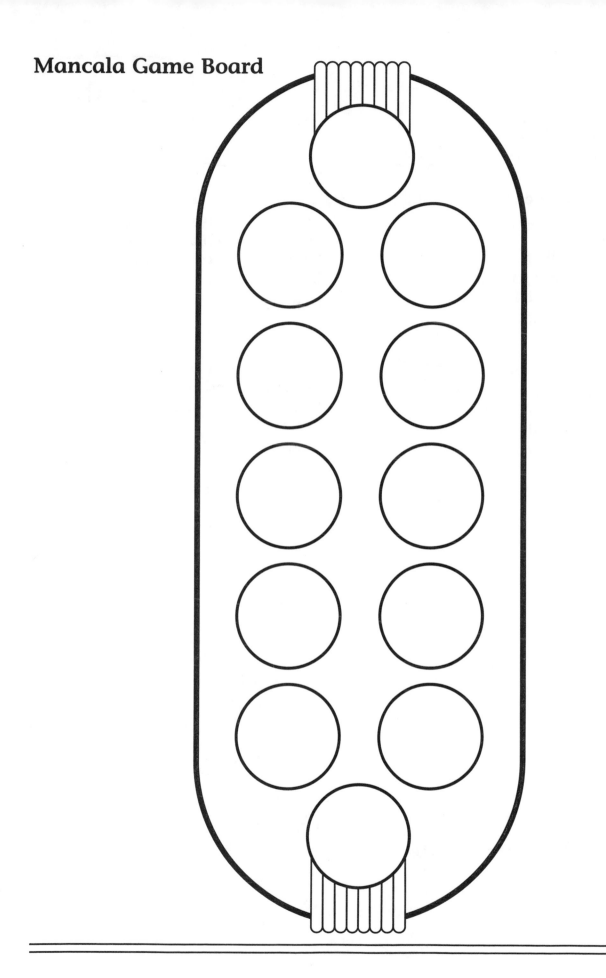

Poison

Skills: Large motor skills and agility

Ages: 7 and older

Players: 8 or more

Materials: Colorful scarf or piece of material tied in a knot

Playground or gymnasium

About the Game

Poisonous berries are often used to dye cloth. The object of this game is to "steal" the cloth which was dyed with the poisonous berries. In some United States schoolyards, this game is called *Steal the Bacon.*

Playing the Game

1. Choose one player to be IT. Have the others make a big circle around IT. Put the "poison" (scarf) on the ground in the middle of the circle.

2. Next, IT should pick a player to be the THIEF who moves into the circle with IT.

3. Both players try to grab the "poison." The player who grabs the "poison" first runs to the empty spot on the circle left by the THIEF without being tagged by the other player.

4. The person who gets tagged becomes IT for the next round.

Ending the Game

The game ends when everyone has had a turn.

Yote

Skills: Quick thinking, planning and strategy skills

Ages: 7 and older

Players: 2

Materials: Copy of playing board (page 24), or outdoor sandy area where a board can be made

12 playing pieces for each player: two kinds of dried beans, pebbles and small sticks

About the Game

Yote is a popular game in West African countries, particularly Senegal.

To play this game as many African children and adults do, have your students make their own boards in the soft ground or use a tray filled with sand. Playing pieces can be as simple as nature provides: sticks and stones. This game may remind your students of checkers.

Playing the Game

1. If playing outside, on the ground have players scoop out five rows with six holes in each row. Have each player find 12 playing pieces, either small sticks or pebbles.

2. Players take turns placing one playing piece in any hole—only one piece may be in a hole at a time. It's up to the players if they wish to place all their pieces on the board before they start moving. *Note: For beginners, it may be easier to have them dole out all their pieces before moving.*

3. To move, players take turns taking one piece from a hole and moving it in a straight line (no diagonal moves) to an empty hole.

4. A player captures his opponent's piece by jumping over it and into an empty hole. To capture an opponent's piece, players jump over an occupied hole to land in an empty hole. After a player captures one piece, he or she is allowed an extra point and can remove any one of the opponent's pieces from the board.

Winning the Game

Be the first player to capture all the opponent's pieces.

Yote Game Board

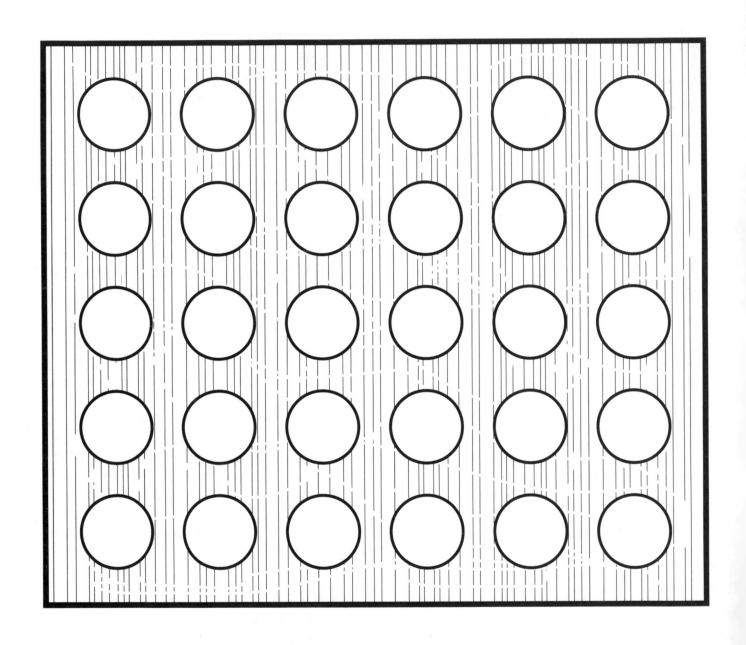

ASIA

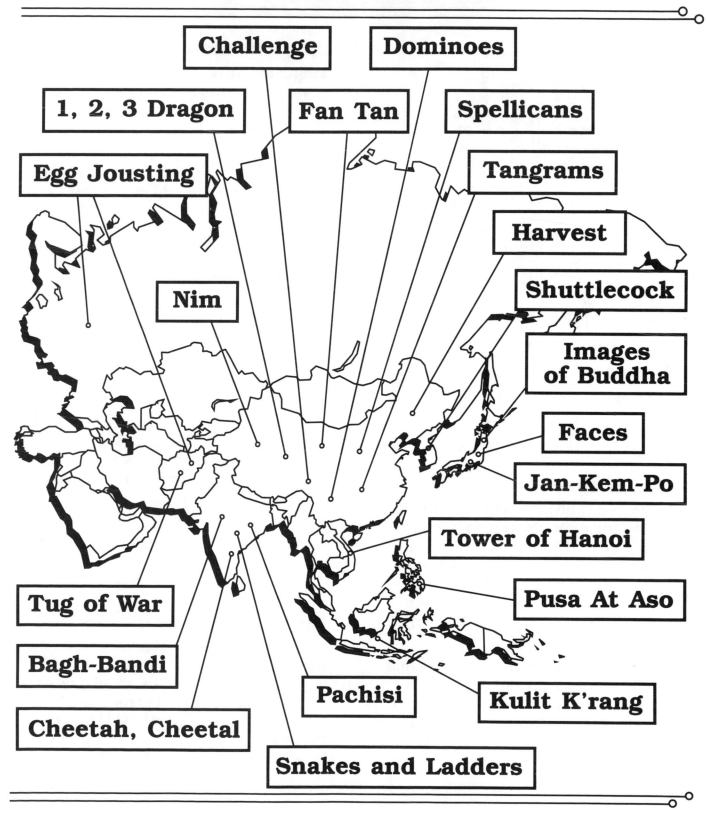

Challenge

Dominoes

1, 2, 3 Dragon

Fan Tan

Spellicans

Egg Jousting

Tangrams

Harvest

Shuttlecock

Nim

Images
of Buddha

Faces

Jan-Kem-Po

Tower of Hanoi

Tug of War

Pusa At Aso

Bagh-Bandi

Pachisi

Kulit K'rang

Cheetah, Cheetal

Snakes and Ladders

Egg Jousting

Skills: Predicting

Ages: 7 and older

Players: 2

Materials: Hard-boiled eggs

Vegetable dyes to color and decorate the eggs

About the Game

Spring is a time for celebration when plants and animals seem to be coming back to life. In many countries, eggs symbolize this new, pure life. Children in Russia, Afghanistan, and Syria usher in spring by playing games during the season's festivals. *Egg Jousting* is one of these popular games.

In these countries, red is the traditional color for dying eggs. Since food coloring isn't available in many places, these children make their dyes from foods such as onions or beets.

Playing the Game

1. Provide each jouster with an equal number of hard-boiled eggs to decorate. It's important that the eggs aren't cracked.

2. Have players play a round of *Mora* (page 80) to decide who goes first. The player who wins will be the CHALLENGER.

3. Jousting terms: Small, pointed end of the egg is called the *head*; larger, rounded end is the *heel*.

   The CHALLENGER faces the OPPONENT and says: "With my head I will break your heel;" or "With my heel I'll break your head;" or "With my head I'll break your head;" or "With my heel I'll break your heel."

4. If the OPPONENT feels he or she can win the challenge, he or she responds: "Then break it," and holds the egg in the palm of the hand with thumb and finger circling the egg.

5. The CHALLENGER takes his or her egg and with the heel or head end up (depending on the challenge) and cracks it down on the OPPONENT'S egg.

Ending the Game

If the OPPONENT'S egg cracks, he or she wins this round, and the OPPONENT'S egg is turned over and the challenge continues. If the egg doesn't crack, the OPPONENT becomes the new CHALLENGER. Players keep score by the number of heads or heels they crack. Eat the eggs when play is over.

Tug of War

Skills: Large-muscle coordination, balancing and strategy skills

Ages: 8 and older

Players: 2

Materials: A baseball bat or a wooden board, approximately 3 feet (1 meter long), all edges sanded smooth

Small outdoor playing area or gym

About the Game

Originally, *Tug of War* was a dramatization of the battle between nature's good and evil forces. Today, in many countries around the world, it is a test of strength. In Burma, the opposing sides represent rain and drought, and the custom is to allow the rain side to win.

Canadian Eskimos hold Tug of Wars to predict winter weather. While in Korea, different villages often gather and play to predict who will have the best harvest. The following Tug of War is played in Afghanistan.

Playing the Game

1. Players draw a line on the ground and stand on opposite sides of the line facing each other.

2. Each player grasps the board. The object is to pull your opponent across the line.

Winning the Game

The player who pulls their opponent across the line is the winner.

1, 2, 3 Dragon

► PLACE OF ORIGIN ◄
China

Skills: Large motor skills, cooperation and quickness

Ages: 8 and older

Players: 10 or more

Materials: Playground or gymnasium

About the Game

This is a great game to play at the beginning of Chinese New Year. The Chinese often welcome in the New Year with colorful parades that feature a colorful, dancing dragon. For the Chinese, the dragon is a symbol of good fortune.

Playing the Game

1. Have players form a line. Ask each player to put his hands on the shoulders of the player in front. The first person in line is the dragon's HEAD, the last person is its TAIL.

2. To start the game, the TAIL shouts out: "1, 2, 3 dragon!" With the HEAD leading and everyone else holding on, the dragon starts to run—twisting and turning trying to catch its TAIL. As the dragon runs after its TAIL it must be careful not to let the body break.

3. If its body breaks, the dragon dies, the HEAD moves to the end of the line and becomes the TAIL, and the person next in line becomes the new HEAD.

Winning the Game

Points are scored each time the HEAD tags the TAIL. The player with the most points wins. Keeping score is fun, but isn't necessary since most players will probably be too tired to keep track of their points.

Challenge

Skills: Quick reactions, addition and subtraction

Ages: All ages

Players: 2

Materials: None

About the Game

This game is a variation of *Odds and Evens* and *Ampe* (see page 16), both popular games in the United States and Ghana, respectively.

Playing the Game

Players face each other and shake their fists as they count to two. On "three," they shout out the number of total fingers they think will be showing. The person closest to the correct number wins one point.

Winning the Game

The first person to win 11 games (or score 11 points) is the winner.

Note: Playing in small groups makes the game more challenging.

Dominoes

Skills: Concentration, math and planning skills

Ages: 6 and older

Players: 4

Materials: Set of 28 dominoes

About the Game

Many have traced the origin of *Dominoes* to China, nearly 2000 years ago, where the "bones," as they were often called, were used as tools to tell the future. More often, however, the bones were used in games to represent the throws of a pair of dice. Chinese sets have 32 bones: 21 which stand for the throws of the dice, and 11 duplicates.

But some historians believe the game may have originated in Egypt where a set of dominoes was found in King Tut's tomb. The young ruler was buried in 1352 B.C. The game, along with a variety of other "common" objects, is believed to have been placed in his tomb "to guide him on his journey through death."

During the fourteenth and fifteenth centuries, Venetian traders to China learned of the game and introduced it to different European communities. For hundreds of years, dominoes have been popular with the working classes as a substitute for playing cards—which, at one time, were very expensive to make and buy.

Dominoes were originally made from materials like bone, wood, and ivory which were inexpensive, easy to carve, and long-lasting. The European domino set has 28 pieces.

Domino terms:

Bones = dominoes

Boneyard = pile of dominoes

To draw = pick dominoes from the pile

Match = two dominoes with the same number of dots

Block = to play a piece that prevents an opponent from taking a turn

Starting the Game

To decide who goes first or is the leader: Players draw one domino from the pile, the person with the highest number wins.

Blind Hughie

Playing the Game

1. Spread the dominoes face down. Without turning over the pieces, each player picks five dominoes and places them face down in a straight row, in front of his or her spot.

2. Draw to see who will be the leader. The leader takes his or her leftmost domino and places it in the center of the table, face up.

3. Moving clockwise, each player turns his or her leftmost domino over. If one side matches the lead piece, the person plays it; if it doesn't match, the domino is turned face down and placed on the right side of his or her row.

Winning the Game

The first one to use up his or her tiles, wins. If no one can move, the game is a draw.

Matador

Playing the Game

1. The object of this game is to join ends that match *and* add up to seven. The *Matadors* are the "free or wild" cards. They are the double blank, and the pieces with the dots totaling seven (6–1, 5–2, 4–3).

   Note: These are used when a player cannot add a domino that adds up to seven.

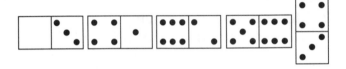

2. Draw to see who goes first. Each player takes five dominoes and lines them up so only they can see their pieces.

3. The leader places one domino in the center of the table. The player to the leader's right puts down a piece that when added to one end of the first piece equals seven. If that player cannot add to the line, that player must draw from the boneyard until he or she can add to the line.

4. Play continues to the right.

Winning the Game

The first to play all of his or her dominoes, wins the game. In the case of a draw—when no one can make another move—each player adds up the dots on their dominoes. The person with the lowest score wins.

Sebastopol

Playing the Game

1. Each player takes seven dominoes and lines them up so only they can see their own pieces.

2. The person with the double sixes leads and places that piece in the center of the table. Play continues to the right of the leader.

3. The next four dominoes which are placed down *must* have a six in them. Players lay them down to form a cross (see picture).

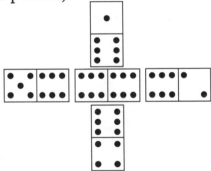

   If a player doesn't have a six, he or she passes.

4. Players continue the game by making matches with the ends. If a match is made, play is passed to the next player.

Winning the Game

The first to play all of his or her dominoes, wins the game. In the case of a draw— when no one can make another move— each player adds up the dots on their dominoes. The person with the lowest score wins.

Fan Tan

Skills: Probability, counting, and estimating skills

Ages: 7 and older

Players: Any number

Materials: Paper

Stick, chopstick, pencil or other stick-like object

Bag or bowl of dried beans

About the Game

This number game is played in Chinese communities around the world. It's a great game for children to practice their counting and estimating skills.

Playing the Game

1. Have students number the corners of a piece of paper 0 through 3 (one number per corner). Each player then picks a number between 0 and 3 and writes his or her initials next to that number on the paper.

2. One player takes a handful of beans and places it on the paper. Using a chopstick, the beans are counted out into four piles.

3. Play stops when beans can no longer be distributed equally.

Winning the Game

The person whose number matches the number of beans remaining is the winner.

Harvest

Skills: Imagination, sequencing, speed and agility skills

Ages: 7 and older

Players: 6 or more (the larger the group the better)

Materials: Outside playing area

Optional: hoe, watering can, fake vegetables/fruit, bucket, basket

About the Game

Harvest time has always been a time of great importance. This is when the year's work will finally pay off. It is a time of cooperation, where everyone, from the youngest to the oldest, pitch in. Our own school calendar is based on harvest time. During summers, schools closed primarily so children could help on the family farm. This game is played in China. It's all about cooperation—working together to get the job done as quickly and efficiently as possible.

Playing the Game

1. Divide players into two teams. Pick one player from each team to be the FARMER to oversee the work and make sure it is done properly. Assign each of the other players a task such as hoeing, planting, weeding, watering, fertilizing, picking. *Note: Players must complete the task in the order it would actually happen.*

2. Set up the "garden" on one end of the playing field and have players line up on the other end forming two lines. On "Go!" the first player in each line runs to the garden, does his or her task, runs back, and tags the next person in line.

Winning the Game

The first team to prepare the land, plant the crop, and harest the fruit, wins. Add to the game by playing music or singing work songs.

Nim

Skills: Counting, creative thinking and planning skills

Ages: 8 and older

Players: 2

Materials: 16 toothpicks, beans, or other small markers

About the Game

This is the thousand-year-old Chinese game of *Nim*. It doesn't have any set patterns or rules. Here, however, is one way it might be played.

Playing the Game

1. Players will need 21 toothpicks or other small game pieces. Arrange the sticks in one row as shown in the picture.

2. Taking turns, the players pick up 1, 2, or 3 sticks at a time.

Winnng the Game

The player to pick up the last stick, loses.

Spellicans

Skills: Sharp eyes, steady hands, math, patience, concentration and planning skills

Ages: 8 and older

Players: 2 to 4

Materials: Wooden Pick-up sticks or 50 wooden skewers or very thin dowels

Paint (five different colors)

About the Game

Spellicans were originally made of ivory. The end of each stick was beautifully carved to represent a flower, animal, or tool. The more intricate the shape, the harder it was to pull from the pile, and thus, the more points it would be worth.

Playing the Game

1. Make a set of Spellicans by painting the ends of each stick a color. Before painting, assign points to each color. For instance: Red, 3 points; Blue, 5 points; White, 10 points; Yellow, 15 points; Green, 20 points. Next, divide the sticks into piles—paint the greatest number of sticks red (or the color with the lowest point values).

2. In China, the youngest person gets to "toss" the spellicans by holding them in one hand a few inches above the table before releasing them at once into a pile.

3. Determine who is the oldest player. This person goes first. He or she chooses a stick and must pull it from the pile without disrupting any of the other sticks. If successful, he or she goes again. If another stick moves, the player's turn is over. Play continues clockwise.

Winning the Game

Play continues until all the sticks are pulled. Players total up their sticks: The person with the most points, wins.

Tangrams

Skills: Creative thinking, imagination, spatial development and strategy skills

Ages: 6 and older

Players: 1

Materials: Tangram pattern (page 38)

Cardboard

Ruler

Scissors

Pencil

About the Game

This puzzling game that has no winners or losers is said to have originated in China over two thousand years ago, but no one knows for sure. If your students are at a loss for story ideas, tell them the tale of Tan, the tile maker. The story may have gone something like this:

Tan had just finished a beautiful tile for the Emperor. He was admiring his work when a bird flew in the window. Startled, he dropped the tile. The beautiful tile broke into seven pieces—like the ones that appear in the drawing. Upset, Tan tried to put the tile back together. As he worked, he discovered that the more he turned the pieces, the more shapes and figures he could make. Soon he was using the seven pieces to create trees, birds, fish—everything but the original tile. He used the broken tiles to "illustrate" stories he told to his children.

Approximately 1,600 images can be made with the seven tangram pieces. What are some illustrations your students can make?

Playing the Game

1. To make your own tangrams, reproduce the pattern on the following page and cut along the lines.

2. The object is for players to use their imaginations to create an image of a recognizable figure using all seven pieces. Try making, animals, flowers, people, objects.

3. Another challenge is to have students create as many varied-sided polygons as possible. For instance, working as a team, how many 5-sided figures can they make?

Tangram Pattern

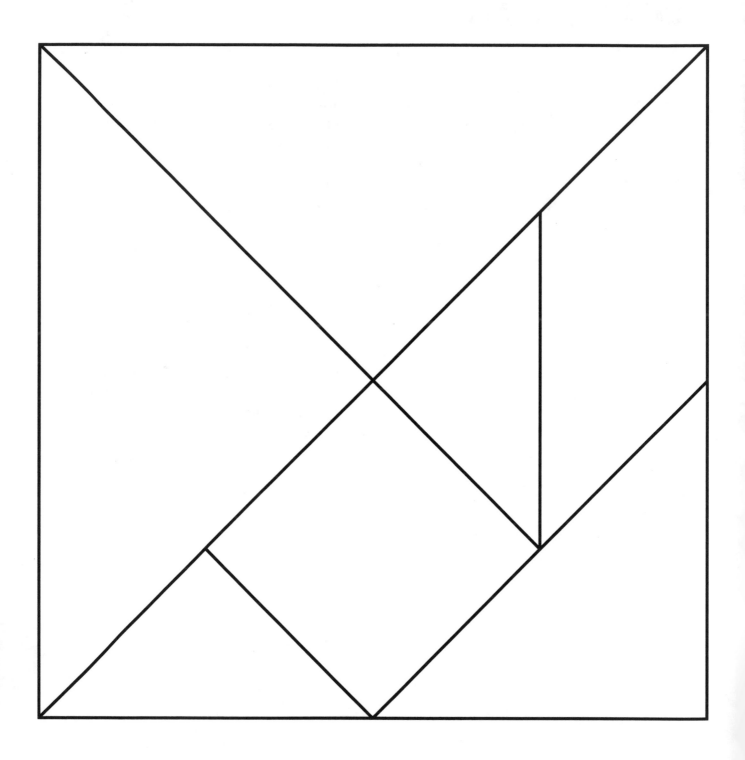

Bagh-Bandi

Skills: Thinking, planning and strategy skills

Ages: 9 and older

Players: 2

Materials: Copy of *Alquerque* game board (page 85)

22 small and stackable playing pieces (20 of one type or color, 2 of different of a different type or color)

About the Game

This is a game of tigers and goats popular in Bengal (a place famous for its tigers). The board is similar to the one used in the Spanish game of *Alquerque*, but the game is played more like *Fox and Geese* where one player has far fewer pieces than another.

Playing the Game

1. One player represents the GOATS, while the other represents the TIGERS. There are 20 GOATS and 2 TIGERS.

2. Place the TIGERS on the spots marked on the game board. Stack the GOATS in four piles of five on their marked spots. Both animals move from intersection to intersection.

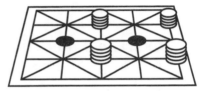

3. GOATS may not eat TIGERS; if a TIGER can jump a GOAT, it must; when a TIGER is cornered and can't move, it is taken off the board.

4. GOATS move one at a time. The top GOAT in the pile moves first. It may only move along a diagonal that is connected to the triangle it starts from.

5. TIGERS make the same moves as the GOAT plus, they can jump a GOAT on its own or in a pile if there is an open spot on the GOAT'S other side. Each time a GOAT is jumped, it is eaten and removed from the board. Only the top GOAT in a pile may be eaten. It is possible for a TIGER to make more than one jump in a move-eating after each jump.

Winning the Game

TIGERS win if they eat all the GOATS.

GOATS win if they corner the TIGERS making it impossible for them to move.

Cheetah, Cheetal

"Chee-eee-eee!"

Skills: Quickness, quick thinking and large motor skills

Ages: 6 and older

Players: 7 or more

Materials: Playing field

Chalk or cones to mark off boundaries

About the Game

For centuries, it has been said that Indian princesses trained cheetahs to hunt *cheetals* (a spotted deer). Although this game of tag got its name from these animals, the cheetahs are not the only ones doing the "hunting."

Playing the Game

1. To make the playing field, draw or mark off two lines about 5 feet (1.5 meters) apart. On either side of these lines, pace off about 20 to 30 feet (6 to 9 meters) and mark off the areas. These are the baselines.

2. Pick one person to be the Indian PRINCESS or PRINCE. Divide the rest of the players into two teams: CHEETAHS and CHEETALS.

3. Have the CHEETAHS and CHEETALS line up, back to back. The PRINCE or PRINCESS stands at the top middle of both lines and calls out, "Chee-eee-ee..." "tah" or "tal" trying to surprise the groups.

4. The team that's called must turn quickly and chase the other players to their baseline. Tagged players are out of the game.

Ending the Game

Play continues until all the players on one side are tagged.

Pachisi

Skills: Counting and hand-eye coordination

Ages: 8 and older

Players: 2 to 4

Materials: Copy of game board (page 43)

4 playing pieces—one colored red, one black, one green, and one yellow.

6 cowrie shells or large dried beans painted on one side (these are the dice)

About the Game

Pachisi is considered to be India's national game. Copies of the cross-shaped game board have been found carved in ancient temples dating back to the 6th century. The name *Pachisi* comes from the Indian word for 25—which is the highest roll on the "dice."

In the 1500s, Moghul Emperor Akbar played Pachisi on a life-size board outdoors—using humans as playing pieces!

Playing the Game

1. On one side of each piece, draw an "X" or other symbol.

2. Each player sits in front of one arm (or *char*) of the board and places a playing piece on the center, which is called the *char-koni*.

3. Players decide who goes first by throwing the cowrie shells. The person with the most shells with their mouths facing up, goes first. The player throws again, this time moving his or her piece according to the number of shells facing up.

How to move using cowrie shells:

6 cowries with their "mouths" facing up—6 moves

5 cowries with their "mouths" facing up—5 moves

4 cowries with their "mouths" facing up—4 moves

3 cowries with their "mouths" facing up—3 moves

2 cowries with their "mouths" facing up—2 moves

1 cowrie with its "mouth" facing up—10 moves, plus another throw

0 cowries with their "mouths" facing up—25 moves, plus another throw

4. Play moves counterclockwise around the board (see the diagram for notes on how to move). Each player moves the number showing from his or her throw down the center of his or her own char and up and around the other chars.

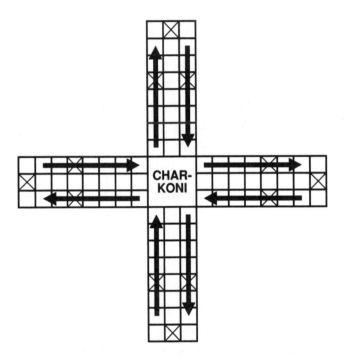

5. When the piece returns to its home char, it is flipped over to show that it has made the path around the board.

6. The piece is moved up its home char toward the center char-koni, which it must reach on an exact throw.

7. As pieces move around the board they may be attacked—unless they are on one of the safe spots, or *castle* squares, marked with an "X." Any number of pieces may rest on a castle square at a time.

8. Pieces are captured when players land on squares occupied by an opponent. Captured pieces are moved back to char-koni and must begin again. The player who captured the piece may move again.

Winning the Game

Be the first to move your counter around the board and back to the char-koni.

Pachisi Game Board

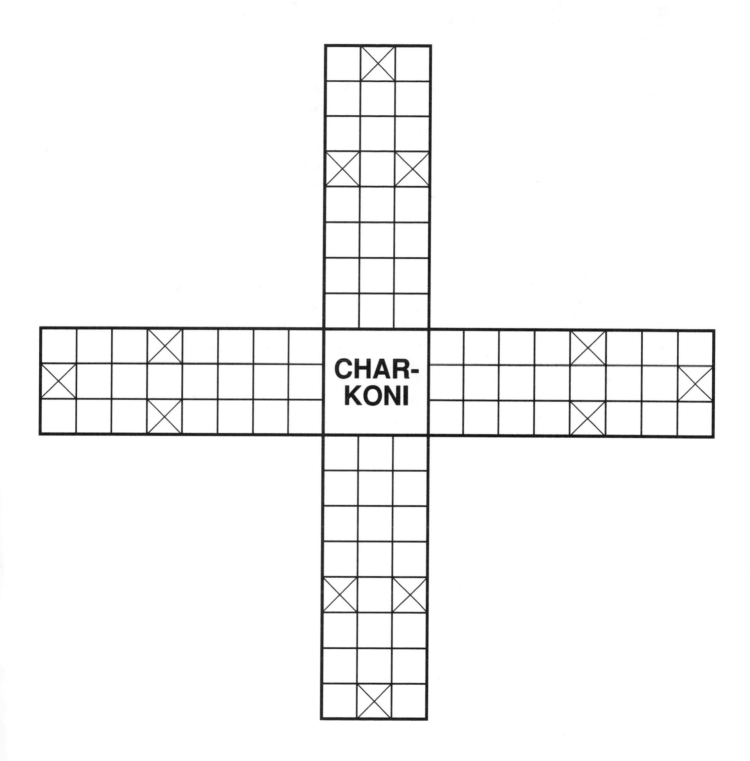

Snakes and Ladders

Skills: Counting and hand-eye coordination

Ages: 7 and older

Players: 2 to 4

Materials: Copy of game board (page 45)

Different colored counter for each player

One or two dice

About the Game

Snakes and Ladders is based on an Indian game called *moksha-patamu*. The game represents a human's "moral journey through life." Based on the Hindu belief of reincarnation, good and evil exist in all people, but the acts of goodness are those that will be rewarded in another life. For instance, a person will "come back" wealthier and with more good things than they had in their first life. In the game, acts of goodness are rewarded by a trip up a ladder to a safe spot.

But acts of evil or wrongdoing are punished. According to the religion, an evil doer will be reincarnated as a lower life form, such as an animal. On the game board, snakes represent evil, and always lead to an animal.

In Western cultures, the game has no religious significance, and is instead a table-top obstacle course.

Playing the Game

1. To begin, a player must roll a six with one die or a double with two dice. The player rolls again and moves the number showing on the dice, beginning on square 1.

2. If a player's counter lands on the head of a snake by exact count the player slides down its body and begins in the space occupied by its tail. If the counter lands on the bottom of a ladder by exact count, the player climbs it to the top square.

3. An exact throw is needed to land on square 100. If the player over rolls, he or she must move backward for each extra number.

Winning the Game

The first player to land on square 100, wins.

Snakes and Ladders Game Board

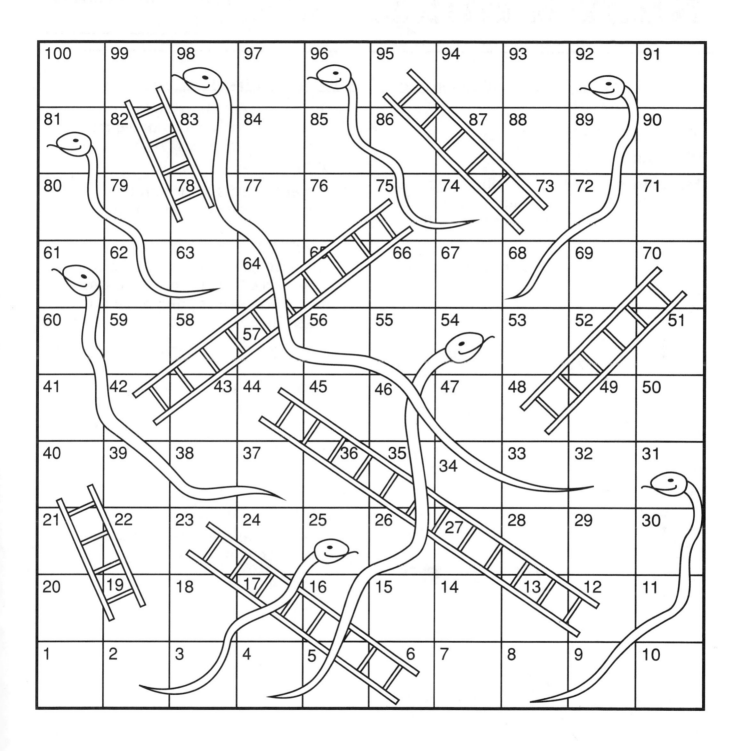

Kulit K'rang

Skills: Hand-eye coordination and speed

Ages: 8 and older

Players: 6 or more

Materials: Pebbles, seashells, dried beans (enough to give each player 10–15 pieces, with about 20 for the bowl)

Basket, box, or plastic bowl

About the Game

Children in Indonesia and other parts of Southeast Asia play this game with *cockleshells*—a small type of seashell. It takes a lot of coordination and quick reflexes to master. The larger the group, the more fun the game is.

Playing the Game

1. Have players form a circle around the bowl. Give each player an equal number of playing pieces (10–15). Leave 20 in the bowl.

2. Players sit cross-legged and pile their pieces in front of them. The first player places a piece on the back of his or her hand. With a quick motion, he or she tosses the piece into the air, grabs another piece from his or her pile and then catches the falling piece—all at the same time.

3. If a player succeeds in snatching and catching the piece, he or she takes one piece from the bowl. If the player fails, he or she adds a piece to the bowl.

4. Play continues to the right until all are out of pieces or when the bowl is empty.

Winning the Game

The player with the most pieces when the game is over, wins.

Faces

Skills: Small motor skills, self-esteem and directional skills

Ages: 7 and older

Players: 2 or more

Materials: Light cardboard (enough to cover the face)

Felt-tipped markers

Scissors

String

About the Game

The art of portrait painting in Japan has been around for ages. Japanese children are often taught to paint using special camel-hair brushes—the same brushes they use to make the fine strokes needed for writing. This game encourages children to be creative and to be able to accept, with good humor, their "creations" of themselves.

Playing the Game

1. Give each child a piece of cardboard. Let them cut it into any shape they want. This will be their mask or "face" canvas.

2. Poke a hole on either side of the mask. Loop a piece of string through each hole to tie the cardboard over the player's face.

3. Have one person be the leader. The leader instructs players to use one marker to draw. The leaders says: "Draw *your* mouth." or "Draw *your* right eye."

4. When their faces are finished, without looking at their creations, have them write their names on the backs.

Ending the Game

Children identify which face belongs to them.

Images of Buddha

Skills: Memory and creative thinking

Age: 7 and older

Players: 5 or more

Materials: None

About the Game

In the Buddhist religion, Buddha is a symbol of virtue and wisdom, who is well known and respected. Buddha has been carved in over 500 different positions. For example, Buddha may be seen laughing with his hands in the air, or sitting with his hands on his thighs, and even playing musical instruments. Here's a game Japanese children play to mimic Buddha's many poses.

Playing the Game

1. Players stand in a circle and face each other. Each person strikes a different pose. Together they say this poem:

   Rakansan, rakansan, rakansan ga,
   Sorottara-soro soro
   Hajime ya janaika
   Yorija, so no so
   Yorija, so no so.

2. As the last line is said, everyone takes the pose of the person to his or her left.

3. Players continue repeating the poem and changing poses. Only one person may strike a particular pose at a time. If a player doesn't take the pose of the person next to him or her, the player is out of the game.

Ending the Game

Play continues until only one person is left in the circle.

Jan-Kem-Po

Skills: Quick reactions and small-muscle skills

Ages: All ages

Players: Any number

Materials: None

About the Game

Jan-Kem-Po is the Japanese version of Paper-Scissors-Rock. In Japan, the game is a match of speed and agility not to mention a little luck, too. It is played as a game by school children and as a method for deciding who goes first, second, third, and so on, by both children and adults.

Playing the Game

1. In this game *Jan* represents rock (a closed fist), *Kem* represents paper (a flat hand), and *Po* represents scissors (two fingers in a V).

2. Similar to the United States' game, the following are winning combinations:
   - ROCK breaks SCISSORS (closed fist beats two-fingered V);
   - SCISSORS cut PAPER (two-fingered V beats flat hand); and
   - PAPER covers ROCK (flat hand beats closed fist).

3. Have all players stand close together in a circle. Choose one person to be the leader. The leader makes a fist with one hand and pumps it twice saying *jan, kem*, on the third time, the leader shouts *po*, and all the players throw out their hands making rock, paper, or scissors.

4. The object is to beat the leader.

Winning the Game

The first player to do this three times wins and becomes the new leader.

Shuttlecock

Skills: Balance, agility and large muscle skills

Ages: 8 and older

Players: 1 or more

Materials: Play area

Small rubber ball or cork ball

10 feathers

Glue (Super Glue or equivalent works best)

Nail or drill

Ping-Pong paddles (optional)

About the Game

This game has been played in Korea, China and Japan for over 2,000 years. In Korea, the game was popular with street venders and store owners who spent a lot of time in the cold. They played *Shuttle-cock* alone or with each other to keep their feet warm. At one time in Japan it was used to train and sharpen a soldier's muscle skills. And in Sixteenth Century England, young girls played a version of Shuttlecock using paddles. As they bounced the ball they recited poems about each other's futures. Here's one:

Shuttlecock, shuttlecock, tell me true,
How many years have I to go through?
One, two, three. . .

Playing the Game

1. To make the shuttlecock, nail or drill a cluster of ten small holes in the ball. Put a drop of glue on each feather's pointed end and insert it into a hole in the ball.

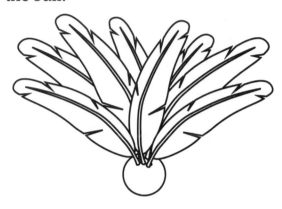

2. Play begins when the shuttlecock is thrown up in the air. On it's way down, the player "catches" it off any part of his or her foot and kicks it back up. To keep score, count the number of times the shuttlecock is kicked in a row without touching the ground. Same rules apply for solo and group Shuttlecock.

3. Add Ping-Pong paddles and the game turns into *Battledore*. Have players count how many times they can bounce the shuttlecock without dropping it. This is also a good time to introduce some counting poems.

Pusa At Aso

Skills: Speed and agility

Ages: 6 and older

Players: 10 or more

Materials: None

About the Game

Puso at aso means cat and dog in the Filipino language of Tagalog. This game is guaranteed to get students' blood pumping, particulary for the two named cat and dog. *Puso at Aso* also teaches children how to work together to have fun.

Playing the Game

1. Choose two players—one to be the DOG, one to be the CAT. Have the other players join hands and make a large circle. The DOG stands on the outside of the circle and the CAT on the inside.

2. On the count of three, the DOG tries to run into the circle and catch the CAT. Both the CAT and DOG may run in and out of the circle at will.

3. Players standing around the circle are there to help the CAT. To prevent the DOG from catching the CAT, players can raise and lower their joined hands making it hard for the DOG to pass by. They can do the same thing for the CAT.

4. If any player around the circle feels the DOG needs a break, the player yells: "Open the gates!" and everyone releases their hands.

Ending the Game

Once the CAT is tagged, he or she returns to the circle and another player is chosen. Players may want to change the rules and have the CAT chase the DOG.

Tower of Hanoi

Skills: Planning, strategy

Ages: 8 and older

Players: 1

Materials: Standard sheet of construction paper

7 circles (ranging in size from 10 inches [25 centimeters] in diameter to 4 inches [10 centimeters] in diameter)

Pencil, pen, crayon, or other writing instrument

About the Game

This puzzle goes by many different names and can be found in many different countries. It is a game of strategy that will puzzle even the sharpest thinkers.

Playing the Game

1. Draw three circles on the construction paper. Label them 1, 2, 3. Stack the circles, beginning with the largest on the bottom, on circle labeled 1.

2. The object is to get the stack from circle 1 to circle 3 in as few moves as possible. The center circle 2 is used only as a holding bin.

3. Disks may be moved from one stack to the other. There are two rules: larger disks may not cover smaller disks and only one disk may be moved at a time.

Winning the Game

The person who transports the stacks with the fewest number of moves, wins.

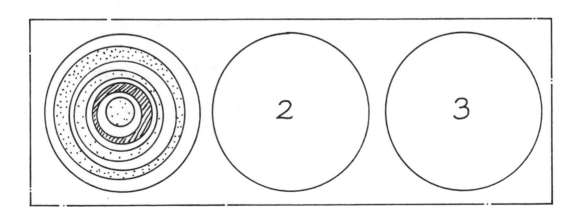

AUSTRALIA

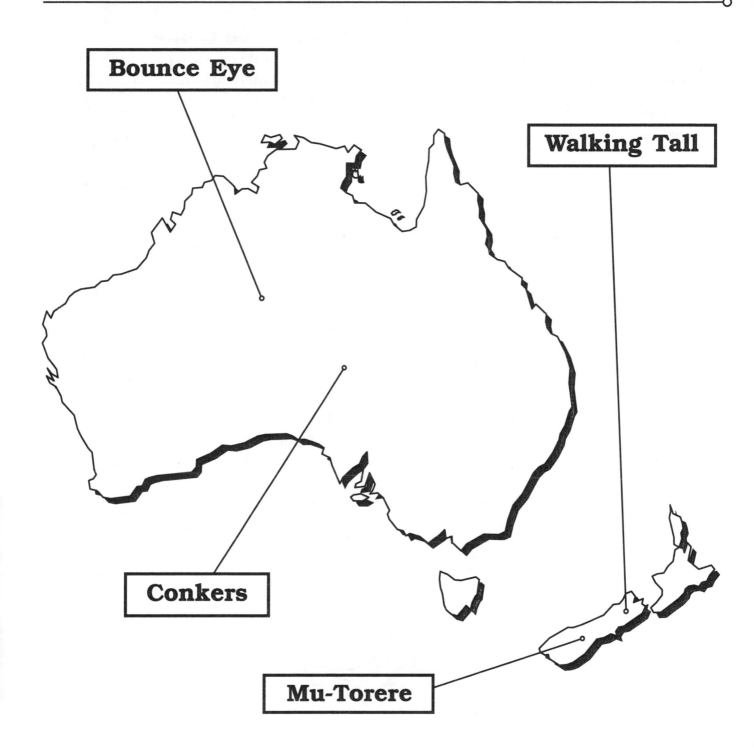

Bounce Eye

Walking Tall

Conkers

Mu-Torere

Bounce Eye

Skills: Small motor skills and hand-eye coordination

Ages: 6 and older

Players: 3 to 4 players

Materials: Playground

3 marbles for each player

Chalk

About the Game

In the mid- to late-1700s, British settlers arrived in Australia. Like the United States, it took years for the new settlers to establish their own society—separate from that of Britain. Here's a game that was invented by those early settlers. The name *Bounce Eye* comes from how the game is played.

Playing the Game

1. Using chalk, create a circle one foot (30 centimeters) in diameter on the playground.

2. Have each player place two of his or her marbles in the center of the circle.

3. Taking turns, each player stands next to the circle, holds his or her marble at eye level and drops it into the center trying to knock the other marbles out of the circle. The player collects all marbles that leave the circle.

4. If no marbles are knocked out, the player leaves his or her marble in the circle and the player's turn is over.

5. Play continues until all marbles are knocked out of the circle.

Winning the Game

The person with the most marbles wins.

Conkers

Skills: Eye-hand coordination and concentration

Ages: 9 and older

Players: 2

Materials: 2 hard, smooth horse chestnuts or hazelnuts

2 sneaker laces

Screw nail or other sharp object for making holes

About the Game

This game is popular with children in Australia, England, and Scotland. Its name—created by the game's players—comes from the word conquerors. To some, *Conkers* is a very serious game. The nuts would be prepared for battle by soaking them first in vinegar or salt water and then drying them out in a warm spot such as the top of a radiator or in an oven. They believed this made the nut tougher and more likely to survive competition. Encourage your students to test these and other methods for strengthening the chestnuts.

Playing the Game

1. Prepare the chestnuts by making a hole through their centers—being careful not to crack the nut. If the nut cracks, it's no good. Thread a string through each hole. Tightly knot one end of the string, so the nut won't slip off.

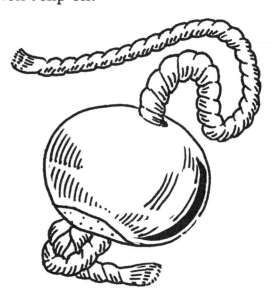

2. To begin, players wrap the free end of their string twice around their hands—about 10 inches (25 centimeters) of string should hang from their hands. The player who is picked to go first, is the CHALLENGER, the other person is the CHALLENGED.

3. The CHALLENGED holds his or her arm out to the side, letting his or her conker hang down. When the conker is still, play begins.

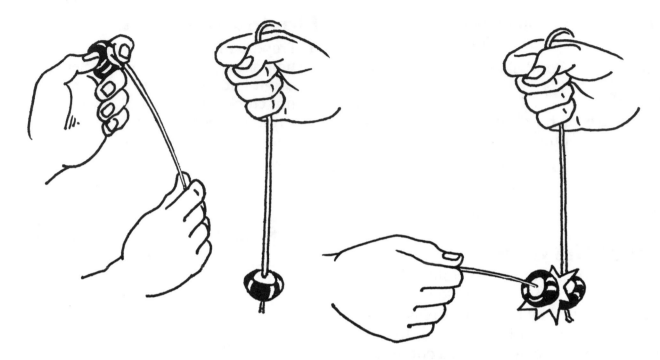

4. The CHALLENGER holds his or her conker in one hand and the opposite end of the string in the other hand. In one fast motion, the CHALLENGER aims and swings his or her conker at the opponent's (the CHALLENGED) conker. The CHALLENGER has three chances to hit the other conker.

5. During the strike, if the strings tangle, the first player to call out "strings!" wins an extra turn.

Winning the Game

Be the first to destroy your opponent's conker. Each time a conker wins, a point is earned. If a conker beats another with previously won points, the points are added to the new winner's points. So a winner with four points who beats another with five points, has 10 points.

Mu-Torere

Skills: Thinking and planning skills

Ages: 6 and older

Players: 2

Materials: Copy of game board (page 58)

8 playing pieces—two different colors

About the Game

The Maoris of Auckland, New Zealand have been playing this game of strategy for hundreds of years. Players learn basic techniques of strategy by carefully planning each move. The game board was originally sketched on the ground or carved into wood. It's simple enough to be drawn on paper.

Playing the Game

1. The eight small circles around the center are called *kewai*. The center circle is called *putahi*. Players begin by placing their pieces on the *kewai* as shown, leaving the *putahi* empty.

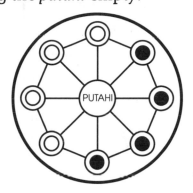

2. There are only a few moves that can be made in this game. They are:

- moving from the *kewai* to the *putahi*;

- moving from the *putahi* to the *kewai*;

- moving from one *kewai* to an adjacent empty *kewai*.

So the only first move a player can make is from a *kewai* next to an opponent's piece to the center *putahi*.

3. Only one playing piece can be on a circle at a time and moves can only be made by pieces which are next to an opponent's piece.

Winning the Game

Players move around the circle trying to block each other. The player to prevent the other from moving, wins.

Mu-Torere Game Board

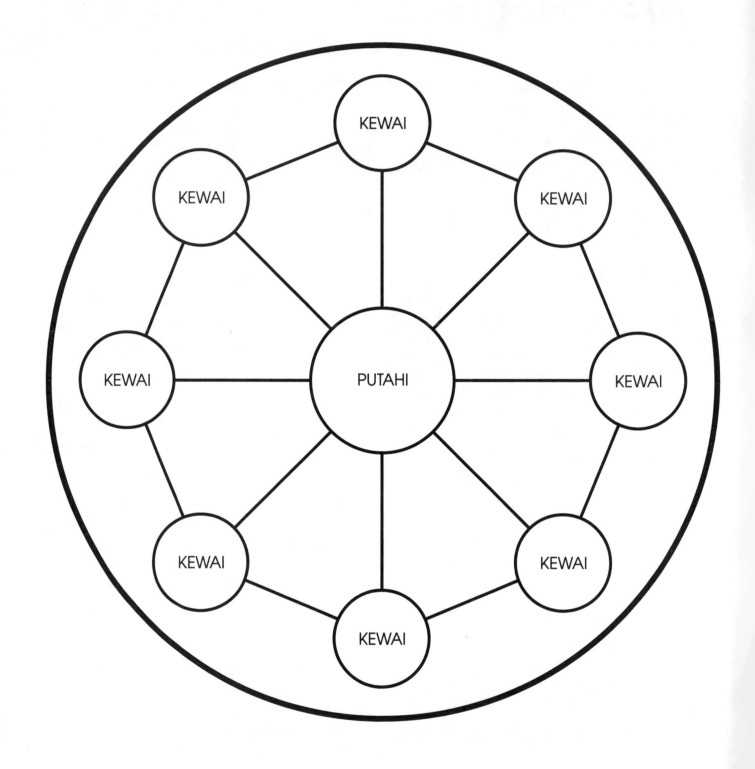

Walking Tall

Skills: Large muscle coordination, balancing and agility

Ages: 8 and older

Players: 1 or more

Materials: To make one set of stilts:

Two 2 in × 2 in × 68 in (5 cm × 5 cm × 173 cm) lengths of wood

Two blocks of wood, 2 in × 2 in × 6 in (5 cm × 5 cm × 15 cm)

Two old tennis balls (to fit over the pole ends)

Wood nails or screws 3.5 in (9 cm) long

Hammer

Outside play area

About the Game

The Maori children of New Zealand play on stilts made from the *manuka*, wineberry tree. Follow the Leader and games of chase (for the more experienced stilt walkers) are often played. In some countries, stilt walkers are traditional parts of parades and festivals—often dressed in fancy costumes.

In some African countries, children are not allowed to use stilts. They are only permitted to be used by tribal priests who walk on them while performing magic rites. In the Landes region of France, shepherds walk on stilts as they tend their animals.

Playing the Game

1. Nail or screw the blocks to the long wooden "sticks" approximately 18 inches (46 centimeters) from the bottom of each stick.

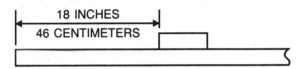

2. Cut a slit in each tennis ball to fit over the top of the long wooden sticks.

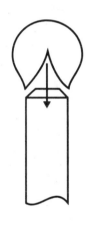

3. The first time stilts are used it may be hard to balance, so have one person stand in front of the person getting up on the stilts to act as a spotter.

4. Once children are comfortable on the stilts they can play games of follow the leader around the playground.

EUROPE

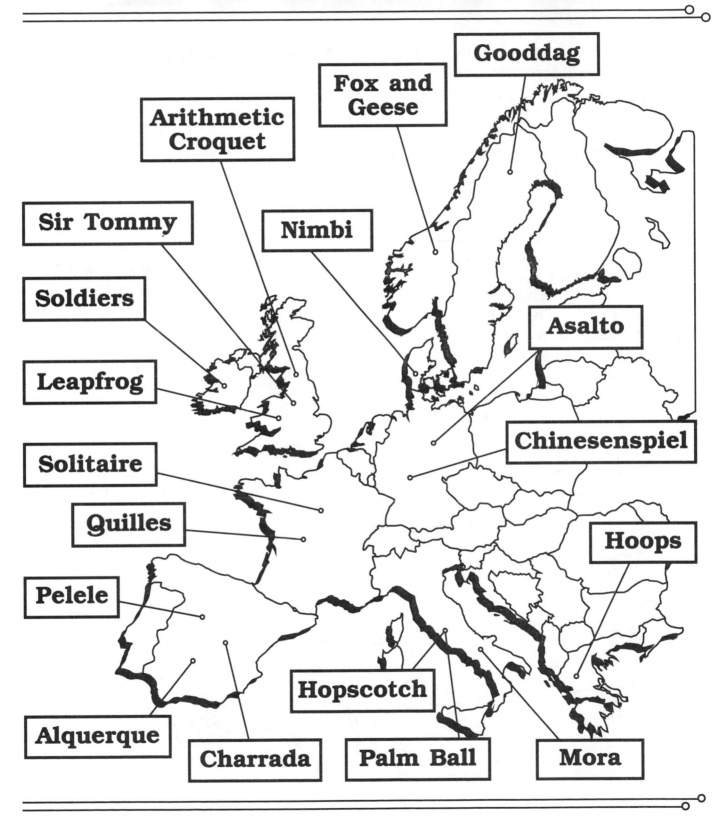

Gooddag

Fox and Geese

Arithmetic Croquet

Nimbi

Sir Tommy

Asalto

Soldiers

Chinesenspiel

Leapfrog

Solitaire

Hoops

Quilles

Pelele

Hopscotch

Alquerque

Charrada

Palm Ball

Mora

Nimbi

Skills: Counting, creative thinking and planning

Ages: 8 and older

Players: 2

Materials: 16 toothpicks, beans, or other small markers

About the Game

This thinking game was developed after a mathematician discovered that the Chinese game of Nim (page 35) could actually be solved with a formula—obviously spoiling the fun. Piet Hein, a Danish mathematician, created this game, that cannot be solved by mathematical formulas, for those extra-sharp thinkers.

Playing the Game

1. Arrange the toothpicks in straight rows and columns—four toothpicks in each.

2. The first player takes any number (up to a total of four) of sticks from any row or column. The only rule is that the sticks must be next to each other.

3. Player two does the same: taking any number (1–4) of toothpicks that are touching, from either a row or column.

Winning the Game

The winner of the game is the person who sets his or her opponent up to take the last stick.

Arithmetic Croquet

▶ PLACE OF ORIGIN ◀

England

Skills: Addition, subtraction and planning

Ages: 7 and older

Players: 2

Materials: Copy of game board (page 64)

Paper

Pencils or pens

About the Game

Mathematician Charles Dodgson and Lewis Carroll, author of *Alice in Wonderland*, have something in common: They are the same person. Carroll loved puzzles and games. In his book, Alice plays an intriguing game of croquet. Here's a game that is equally intriguing, but isn't played with any animals—it's played only with numbers.

Playing the Game

1. Draw 10 wickets down the center of the paper and label them by tens up to 100. On either side of the wickets, make a column to keep score. Label them Player 1 and Player 2 or use the game board provided (page 64).

2. Play a quick game of Jan-Kem-Po (page 49) to decide who goes first.

3. Player one chooses a number between 1 and 8 and writes it down under his or her column. Player 2 chooses a different number between 1 and 8 and writes it in his or her column, with one exception: Player 2's number, when added to Player 1's number, may not total 9.

   For example, if Player 1 picked the number 6, Player 2 may not take the number 3 or 6.

4. Now, to move through each hoop, the player must add the amount it takes to get to the hoop as it does to pass it. For example, if the player picked 7, the next number he or she may write down is 6—it took 3 to get to 10 and 3 to pass it.

5. If a wrong number is used to go through a hoop the player must subtract the number on his or her next turn and continue playing correctly. Remember the same number must be used to move in and out of the hoops.

Winning the Game

The object of the game is to go through the hoops and reach the last hoop (100) with the exact number 100.

If the hoop is missed by going over 100, the player has only one chance left to get it. If the hoop cannot be reached by playing two times, the player loses the game.

Arithmetic Croquet Game Board

PLAYER 1		PLAYER 2
	100	
	90	
	80	
	70	
	60	
	50	
	40	
	30	
	20	
	10	

Leapfrog

Skills: Running and jumping

Ages: 7 and older

Players: 6 or more (the larger the group the better)

Materials: Outside playing area

About the Game

This game is believed to date back to 16th century Britain where everyone from kings and queens to military personnel to townspeople played it. Shakespeare's characters in *Henry V* even played it! Why do your students suppose the game was started? Does the name fit?

Playing the Game

1. Divide players into two teams—forming two lines.

2. On the count of three, the first person in each line should take a running jump. When the players land they should quickly bend over and grab hold of their ankles.

3. As soon as the player is set up, the next person runs and leaps over the first player. When this player lands, he or she should also bend over and grab his or her ankles.

4. Players continue running, leaping, and bending until all players have gone and there is a long line of frogs.

Winning the Game

The first team to finish, wins.

Sir Tommy

Skills: Concentration

Ages: 6 and older

Players: 1

Materials: Standard deck of 52 cards

About the Game

In the United States, card games that are played alone belong to the solitaire family. In England, such games belong to a group called *patience*, probably because that's what they take a lot of to master. *Sir Tommy* is believed to be the father of all solo card games.

Playing the Game

1. The object is to build four piles, or "foundations," which begin with an ace, followed by a 2, and so on, up to king. The cards do not have to be of the same suit.

2. Begin by shuffling the deck. Flip cards one at a time from the deck, or stock pile, into four waste (face up) piles. Aces are used to start the foundation piles—separate from the waste piles.

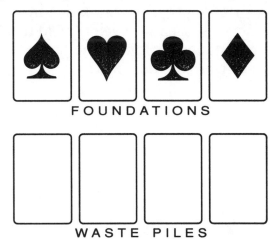

FOUNDATIONS

WASTE PILES

3. The cards from the stock pile may be placed in the waste piles in any order. It's important to think about where the low cards are placed—it's good to avoid placing a high card over one—because once the stock pile is dealt out, that's it.

Winning the Game

Create the most complete foundations: Ace to King.

Solitaire

Skills: Thinking skills

Ages: 8 and older

Players: 1

Materials: Copy of game board (page 68)

32 playing pieces

About the Game

Sentenced to solitary confinement in the Bastille, an 18th century Frenchman created this game to wile away his days. The game spread throughout the prison and eventually made its way to England where it became a very popular parlor game.

Playing the Game

1. Place a playing piece on all black dots—except the center one.

2. To move a piece, the player must jump over a piece and land on an empty dot. Pieces can only be moved by jumping horizontally and vertically.

Ending the Game

The object is to end up with only one piece left on the center dot.

Solitaire Game Board

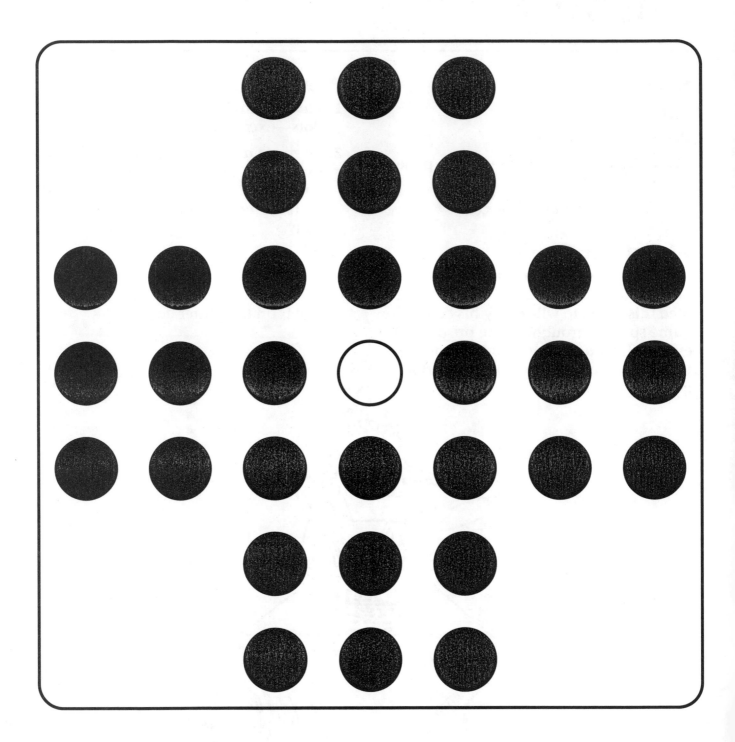

Quilles

Skills: Aiming and math skills

Ages: 8 and older

Players: 2 or more

Materials: Playground with a basketball hoop or tree (where rope can be hung

Rope — 8 to10 feet (2.5 to 3 meters)

Old softball

Screw hook

Ten empty plastic soda bottles (to be used as pins)

Sand, pebbles, or other material to fill soda bottles

About the Game

The first game of *Quilles* was played hundreds of years ago in France. In the late 18th century, Dutch settlers brought it with them to America. Over the years *Quilles* developed into our modern game of bowling.

This game takes more materials and preparation than other games. It is possible to make an indoor table-top version with a little improvising. Making the full-size game as a class will help students understand the teamwork and cooperation that led to success for many of our early settlers.

Playing the Game

1. Insert the screw end of the hook into the softball and tie the hook to the end of the rope. Hang and secure the rope on the basketball hoop.

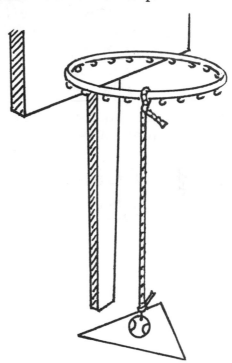

2. Let students fill nine bottles with sand or other materials. Fill the "pins" to different levels with different materials. Later ask students to think about why some "pins" are easier to knock down than others. Fill the tenth "pin" with the most (heaviest) material.

3. Set up the "pins" in a triangle and place the heaviest one in the center directly under the softball.

4. To play, each player aims and swings the ball trying to knock over as many "pins" as possible. One person should stand opposite from the player whose turn it is to catch the ball before it swings back. The ball has only one chance to knock the "pins" over.

5. Scoring: 2 points for outer "pins," 10 points for center "pin."

Winning the Game

After three rounds, the person with the most points at the end is the winner.

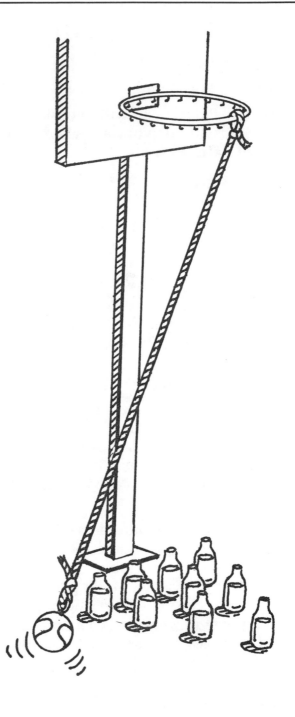

Asalto

Skills: Strategy, thinking and planning skills

Ages: 8 and older

Players: 2

Materials: Copy of game board (page 72)

26 playing pieces (two of which are different from the others)

About the Game

Asalto, or Assault, is a game of strategy that is similar to *Fox and Geese* (page 82) where one side has far fewer pieces than the other. In 1858, this game became known as *Officers and Sepoys*. It is named after the Indian mutiny of 1857, when Indian troops (*sepoys*) revolted against British officers.

Playing the Game

1. One player represents the OFFICERS and has two playing pieces. The other player represents the INDIAN SOLDIERS and has 24 playing pieces.

2. The OFFICERS are placed on any of the points in the fortress (the area marked off by the square). The SOLDIERS are placed on the empty spaces outside the fortress.

3. SOLDIERS may only move in straight or diagonal lines toward the fortress. OFFICERS may move in any direction, and may capture SOLDIERS by jumping over them. If an OFFICER misses a chance to capture a SOLDIER, the OFFICER is taken off the board.

Winning the Game

SOLDIERS win by trapping the OFFICERS anywhere on the board, or by holding every spot in the fortress. OFFICERS win by weakening the SOLDIERS' forces until there are too few left to protect themselves.

Asalto Game Board

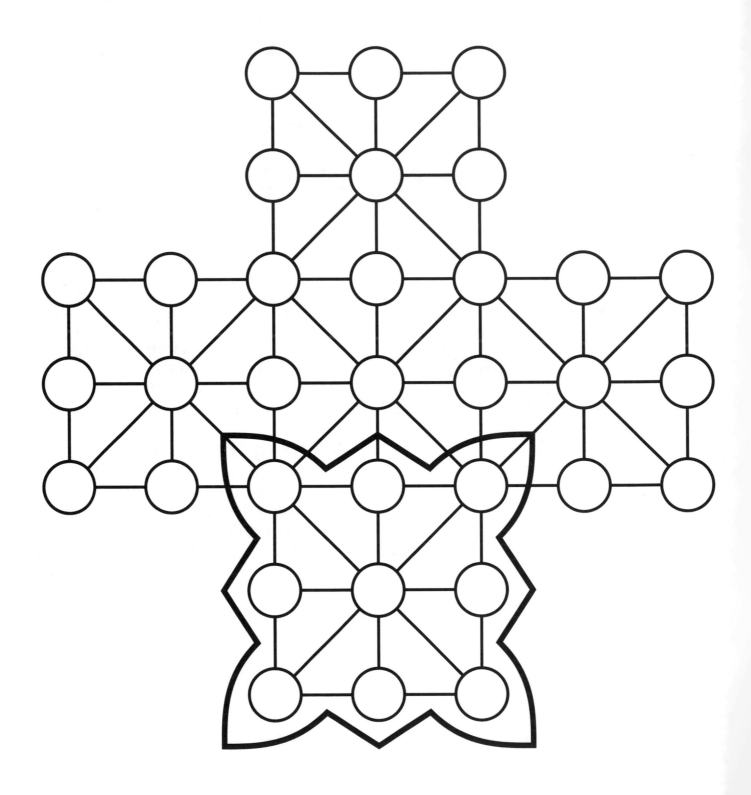

Chinesenspiel

Skills: Strategy skills and understanding of how cultures share information

Ages: 9 and older

Players: 2 to 4

Materials: Copy of game board (page 74)

4 playing pieces: red, blue, yellow, green

Die painted: white on two sides, and red, blue, yellow, and green on the other sides

About the Game

Chinesespiel, or the game of the Chinese, was popular in Germany in the 1800s. At the time, the Germans were very interested in the cultures of both India and China. The game was designed with both cultures in mind: The board was styled after an Indian board game, and the playing pieces were carved to resemble Chinese figures.

Playing the Game

1. Each player places his or her playing piece on the game board corner of the same color.

2. To begin the game, one player rolls the die until a colored side is facing up. The player whose piece matches the die goes first.

3. This player rolls the die. If the color rolled matches the player's piece, he or she moves one space in a counterclockwise direction and rolls again.

4. If a white side is rolled, the player doesn't move, but rolls again. If any color besides the color of the player's piece is rolled, the player's turn is over.

Winning the Game

The first to bring their playing piece around the board, up one of the cross sections, and to the center, wins.

Chinesenspiel Game Board

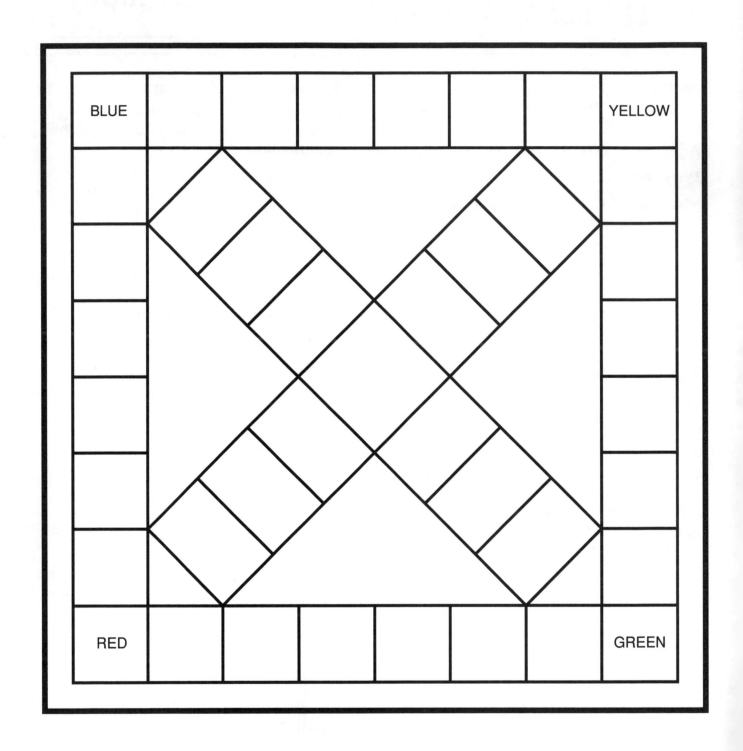

BLUE

YELLOW

RED

GREEN

Hoops

Skills: Concentration, quick and accurate reflexes

Ages: 6 and older

Players: 10 or more

Materials: 2 Hula-hoops

Balls, bean bags, or other objects for throwing

Outdoor playing area or indoor gymnasium

About the Game

Hoop games have been popular since 300 B.C. Over the years, hoops have been used many different ways: Hippocrates prescribed hoop rolling to cure the weak; American Indians used rolling hoops to sharpen young boys' aim; Chugach Eskimos competed by throwing long poles through a moving hoop; European boys and girls participated in hoop-rolling races. In the United States, hula-hoops became a fad of the 1960s.

The Greek philosopher Artemidorus, once wrote: "If you dream about rolling a hoop, it means that you have come to the end of your troubles, and abundant happiness will follow."

Playing the Game

1. Divide players into two teams. Pick one person from each team to be the roller. These two should stand at one end of the playing area.

2. As the rollers roll the hoops past their team, their teammates should try to throw a ball or any pre-selected object through the hoop without touching its sides.

Winning the Game

The team who makes the most successful throws, wins.

Soldiers

Skills: Eye-hand coordination, concentration and math skills

Ages: 9 and older

Players: 2

Materials: Wooden popsicle stick for each player

About the Game

This game was originally played with branches from the ribwort plantain. To win, a player had to knock the end off his opponent's branch with his own.

Playing the Game

1. One player holds his or her popsicle stick by placing one hand on either end. The other player, holds his or her stick with one hand and tries to break the opponent's stick by striking it as hard as he or she can.

2. Players take turns until one person breaks a stick. A point is earned for each stick broken. If a player beats another with previously won points, the points are added to the new winner's points. So a winner with four points who beats another with five points, ends up with 10 points.

Winning the Game

Player with the highest score wins.

Hopscotch

▶ PLACE OF ORIGIN ◀

Italy

Skills: Balancing, aiming and jumping

Ages: 6 and older

Players: 2 to 6

Materials: Playground, sidewalk

Chalk

Game markers: stones for each player

About the Game

The oldest known Hopscotch board is etched into the floor of the Forum in Rome. The game spread throughout Europe by Roman soldiers during the growth of the Roman Empire. Children in Britain, France, and Germany were taught the game by soldiers.

Hopscotch may have developed from myths about mazes and labyrinths—if you study different boards you can see how the game fits into such a story. Some versions of Hopscotch grew from religious beliefs of a human soul's journey from Earth to Heaven.

Hopscotch is one of the most widely played games in the world.

Heaven and Earth

Playing the Game

1. Find a flat space to draw the hopscotch board shown below.

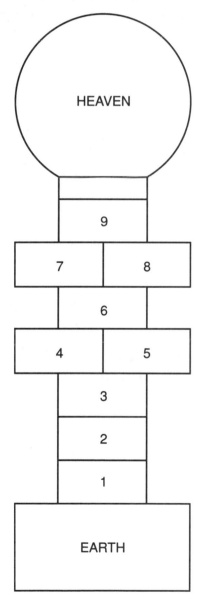

2. The first person begins by standing on "Earth" and tossing his or her marker into box 1.

3. On one foot the player hops into the box 1, bends over, picks up his or her stone, and hops back out—all without letting his or her other foot touch the ground. The player repeats these steps for each box 1–9, always returning to Earth.

4. A player's turn is over if he or she misses the box on a toss, falls, or lands on a line. At his or her next turn, the player begins where he or she left off.

5. Once a player makes it through 1–9, he or she tosses the marker into Heaven.

- **If the marker lands in Heaven**, the player makes the trip from Earth and back. On returning, the player stands on Earth and with his or her back to the board, tosses the marker over his or her shoulder. Upon tossing, **if the marker lands in a box, not on a line**, the player writes his or her initials in the box. From this point on, that box becomes the player's "home"—a place where he or she can put both feet down to rest. Other players must hop over this box.

- **If the marker *does not* land in Heaven**, the player must hop through the board carrying his or her marker, however the other players want the player to. For example, they might have the player rest it on his or her foot, head, back of hand, finger, elbow. Whichever way they choose, the player must balance it on that spot until he or she makes it up and back in one turn.

- **If the marker lands in the Blank Space**, the player must begin his or her turn from the very beginning.

Winning the Game
First player to finish, wins.

Water Hopscotch

Playing the Game

1. Find a flat space to draw the Hopscotch board shown on the right.

2. The strip down the middle of this board is the "water" and is off limits to players and markers. If any part of a player or marker lands in the area, the player is out of the game.

3. The game is played like standard Hopscotch where a marker is tossed first into box 1. The player hops in on one foot, picks up the marker, and hops out. Players do this for each box, always hopping on one foot. From box 5 to box 6, players must hop over the water.

4. Boxes 3, 6, and 9 are designated "rest areas." Players may put both feet down while in these boxes.

5. After making it around to box 10, the player must hop around the entire board three times, on one foot, without resting.

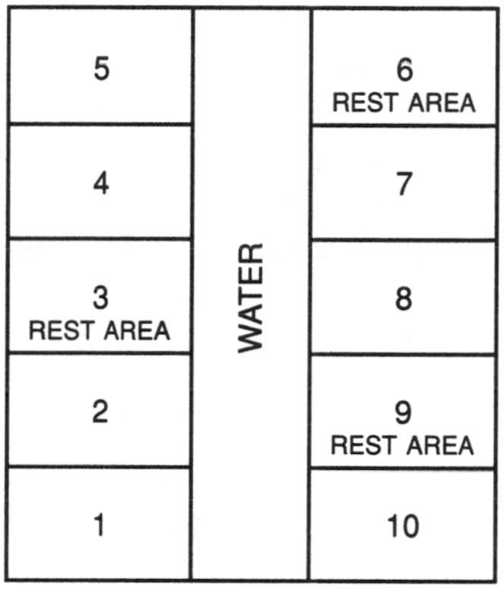

5		6 REST AREA
4		7
3 REST AREA	WATER	8
2		9 REST AREA
1		10

Winning the Game

First player to finish, wins.

Mora

Skills: Counting, quick reactions and language skills

Ages: 7 and older

Players: 2

Materials: Hands

About the Game

Want to learn numbers in a foreign language? This is the perfect game. *Mora* means fingers in Italian. It's an old game originally popular with adults.

Playing the Game

1. Facing each other, players count "One, Two, Three" and then shout out numbers between two and ten. As players shout their numbers, they throw out any number of fingers on one hand.

Winning the Game

The player who accurately guessed the number of total fingers wins.

Variation of the Game

Learning a foreign language? Practice using the numbers below.

English	Italian	Spanish	French	Mandarin	Swahili
One	Uno	Uno	Un	Yi	Moja
Two	Duo	Dos	Deux	Er	Mbili
Three	Tre	Tres	Trois	San	Tatu
Four	Quattro	Cuatro	Quatre	Si	Nne
Five	Cinque	Cinco	Cinq	Wu	Tano
Six	Sei	Seis	Six	Liu	Sita
Seven	Sette	Siete	Sept	Qi	Saba
Eight	Otto	Ocho	Huit	Ba	Nane
Nine	Nove	Nueve	Neuf	Jiu	Tisa
Ten	Dieci	Diez	Dix	Shi	Kumi

Palm Ball

Skills: Aiming and throwing skills

Ages: 7 and older

Players: 2 to 4

Materials: Playground

Tennis or other bouncy rubber ball

Chalk

About the Game

Over two thousand years ago this ancient Roman game began its trek across continents. Brought to Spain by Roman soldiers, the game was quickly picked up and was en route again. This time to America where it became a part of Aztec life. What sport do your students think may have originated from palm ball?

Playing the Game

1. Mark off a large rectangular boundary on the pavement. Draw a line across the middle.

2. Each player or team stands in one half of the box. One player begins by serving the ball to the other side by bouncing it and hitting it with his or her palm. The ball is allowed to bounce once before the other team hits it back over.

3. Points are scored every time a ball is sent out of bounds or missed by a player.

Winning the Game

The first player or team to score 21 points wins.

Fox and Geese

▶ PLACE OF ORIGIN ◀

Norway

Skills: Creative thinking, strategy and planning skills

Ages: 8 and older

Players: 2

Materials: Copy of game board (page 83)

18 total playing pieces: dried beans, coins, chips (one piece must be of a different color from the others)

About the Game

Your students will quickly notice that the opponents in this game aren't equal. There are 17 geese and only one fox. The fox is on the hunt and ready to make a meal out of the geese. Ask your students why a game like this, where there are many against one, started in the Middle Ages.

This is a true game of strategy and is popular—with minor variations—in many countries around the world. For instance, in Japan the game is called, *Juroku Musashi* or *16 Soldiers*. The soldiers in this game try to capture the general. In the United States, this game is played by American Indians in southwestern states. Their game has two variations: A coyote hungry for chickens, and 16 Indians trying to catch a rabbit.

Playing the Game

1. One player is the FOX and the other is the GEESE. Arrange the pieces on the board as shown in the drawing.

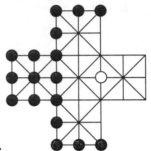

2. Moving:

- FOX always makes the first move. The FOX may move in all directions (forward, backward, diagonally, sideways). It captures GEESE by jumping over them one at a time and landing in an empty space (like checkers).

- GEESE may move in all directions, but backwards. They may *not* jump over the FOX or any other GEESE. The GEESE try to surround the FOX so it can't move.

Winning the Game

FOX must capture enough GEESE so they can't surround him or by out-foxing the GEESE by forcing them to the other side of the board where they can't turn around. GEESE win by surrounding or cornering the FOX so it can't move.

Fox and Geese Game Board

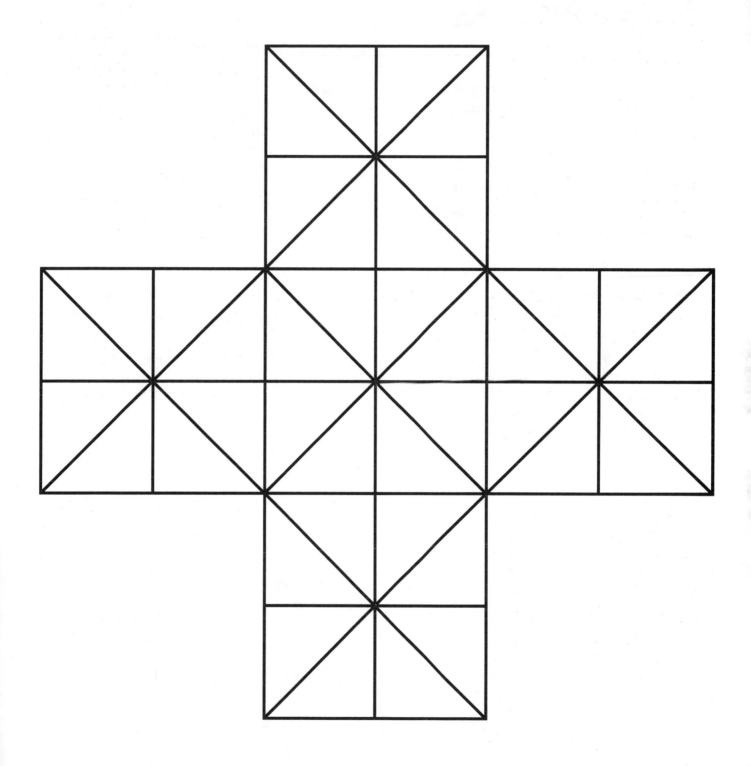

Alquerque

Skills: Thinking skills

Ages: 7 and older

Players: 2

Materials: Copy of the game board (page 85)

12 game pieces for each player, should be two different colors

About the Game

This is the Spanish version of an Arabic game called *El-quirkat*. The game was brought to Spain by the Moors, a group of Arabs who ruled the country from 1000 to 1492. This thinking game is believed to be an early version of *Checkers*. Today, it's not unusual to see people playing a version of *Alquerque* wherever there is enough space to place a board.

Playing the Game

1. Players begin by arranging their pieces on the board as shown by the black and white dots. One player should place his or her pieces on the black dots and the other on the white dots (see diagram below).

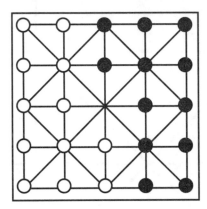

2. Players take turns moving in all directions to adjacent empty spots. Similar to checkers, if an opponent's piece is blocking an empty space, it may be jumped and captured. Players can jump more than one piece at a time.

3. If a player doesn't take the opportunity to jump, his or her piece is captured (removed from the board) by the opponent. If a player has a chance to jump, regardless of the position it leaves him or her in, he or she must do it or be captured.

Winning the Game

Be the first to capture all your opponent's pieces.

Alquerque Game Board

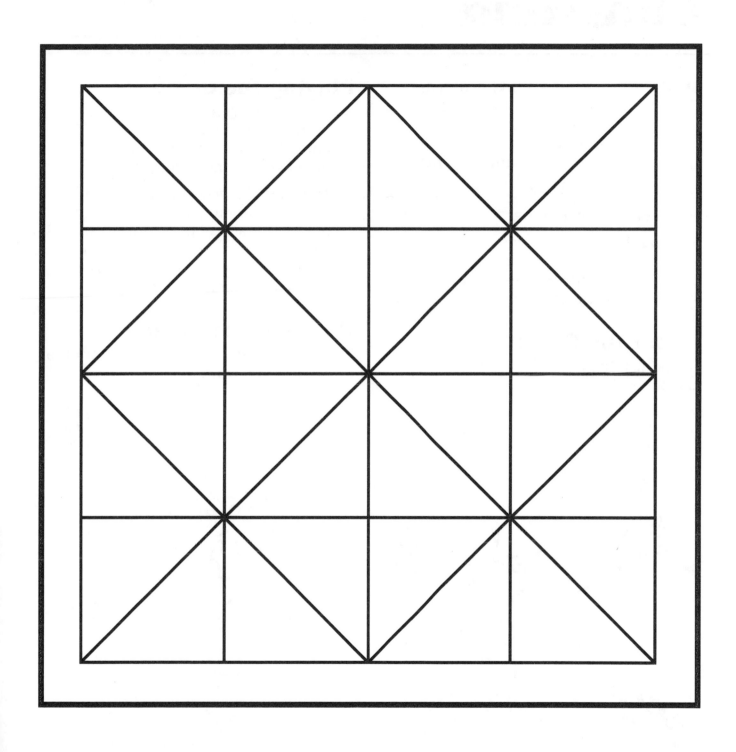

Charrada

Skills: Creative thinking and dramatics, communication through body and facial movements and interpretations and team cooperation

Ages: 7 and older

Players: Any number

Materials: Slips of paper containing selected names, topics, activities, etc. from your unit of study

About the Game

In Spanish the word *charrada* means "the chatter of clowns."

Why do your students think this silent game has such a noisy name? The game of *Charrada* was brought to England around 1775 where it became known as Charades.

Playing the Game

1. Divide players into teams of three or more. Ask one player to pick a slip of paper from the hat and show it to his or her team—the "acting" team.

2. Together, the acting team should decide on a way to act out the information on the slip of paper for the other team. Actors must remain absolutely silent as they play out the word or words for the other teams.

Winning the Game

The first team to accurately shout out the correct answer, wins.

Pelele

Skills: Team work, music, art and creative writing

Ages: 7 and older

Players: 4 or more

Materials: Old pair of child-size pants, shirt, socks, cloth bag

Straw or rags for stuffing

Sewing needle and nylon thread

Paint or felt-tip pens

A big blanket

About the Game

In this game, students learn about ancient rituals and celebrations from *Pelele* (pronounced pay-LAY-lay), a stuffed doll. *Pelele* is used as a symbol for a clown or someone who is not very popular. The stuffed doll is tossed up and down in a blanket as children recite poems ushering in the first days of spring.

Alaskan Eskimos play a similar game but use a real person. Their blanket-toss game is called *Nalukatok*. A person gets tossed in the air and on the way down he tries to land on his feet before getting tossed back up.

Playing the Game

1. To make Pelele, stuff the clothing and sew it together to make a little "person." Draw a face on the cloth bag, stuff it, and attach it to the body. Your students may want to add "hair" and other articles to personalize the doll.

2. Let everyone hold a part of the blanket. Toss Pelele into the center and at the same time, signal players to lift the blanket and toss the doll into the air. Each time he lands back in the blanket, toss him back up again.

3. Encourage students to make up chants and poems to shout out as Pelele flies through the air. Here's one in Spanish:

Pelele, Pelele	Pelele, Pelele
Tu madre te quiere,	Your mother loves you,
Tu padre tambien,	And your father too,
Todos te queremos.	We all love you!
Arriba con el!	Up with him!

Gooddag

Skills: Large motor skills and spatial relationships

Ages: 7 and older

Players: 10 or more

Materials: Playground

About the Game

In Swedish, *gooddag* means Good day! The game is a little like our American game of *Duck, Duck, Goose*. It's often played at the beginning of the school year as a way for children to get acquainted. Because of its name and easy rules, it's also a fun way to introduce special words from a culture students are studying.

Playing the Game

1. Players hold hands and form a big circle. One player is named IT.

2. IT runs around the circle and taps one person on the shoulder. This person and IT run in opposite directions. The other players leave this person's spot open.

3. When the players meet, they shake hands and say to each other *"Gooddag,"* and then race in opposite directions to the empty spot.

4. The player to reach the spot first is safe, the other player is the new IT.

5. This is how you say Good day! in other languages:

   Buenos Días —Spanish

   Bonjour—French

   Guten Tag—German

   Ni Hao Ma—Manderin

   Salamu—Swahili

NORTH AMERICA

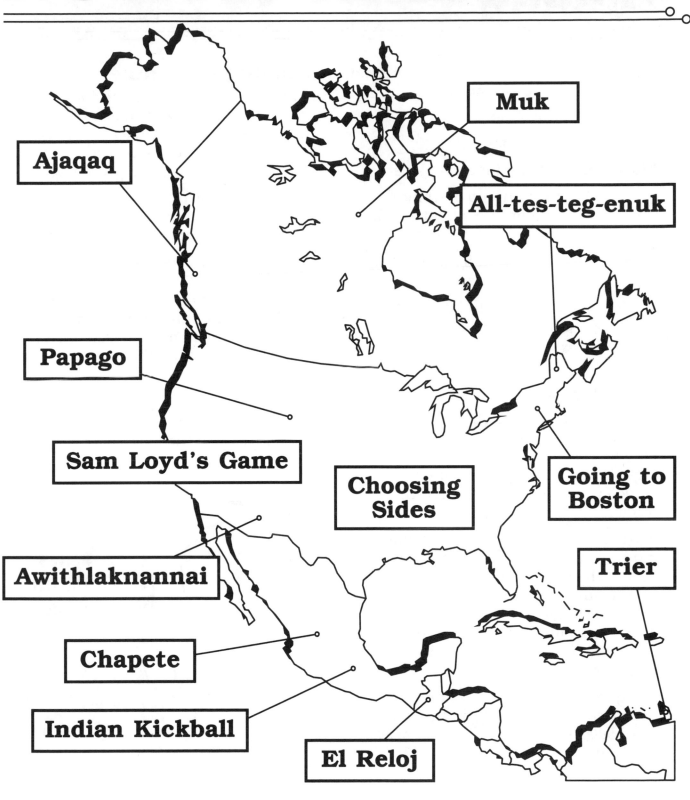

Muk

Ajaqaq

All-tes-teg-enuk

Papago

Sam Loyd's Game

Choosing Sides

Going to Boston

Awithlaknannai

Trier

Chapete

Indian Kickball

El Reloj

Ajaqaq

Skills:	Small motor skills and hand-eye coordination
Ages:	7 and older
Players:	2 or more
Materials:	One set for each player:
	Curtain ring or similar weight ring, about 2 inches (5 centimeters) in diameter
	Stick about 8 inches (20 centimeters) long
	String about 20 inches (50 centimeters) long
	Tape

About the Game

The Eskimos on the northwest coast of Canada have a variety of games they play to wile away the long, dark winter days. It was once believed that playing *Ajaqaq* would make the sun return sooner.

A variety and an abundance of man-made resources are often limited in the Arctic. The people living in these regions take advantage of all natural materials available to them—particularly animals. Bones and muscles from small animals caught for food are traditionally used to make this game.

The game also goes by the name of *Bilboquet* which comes from the French word *bille*, a wooden ball, and *bocquet*, the point of a spear.

Playing the Game

1. Have each player tie one end of the string around the ring and one end around the stick. Tape the string down to prevent it from slipping.

2. Holding the stick in one hand, have them flip the ring into the air and try to catch it on the stick. Players score a point every time they catch the ring.

3. To make play more challenging, have players stand on one foot, use their opposite hands, or try it with their eyes closed. Or let children experiment with an assortment of ring sizes. Players will soon discover the game is harder than it looks.

Winning the Game

The player with the most points wins.

Muk

Skills: Concentration, self control and imagination

Ages: All ages

Players: Any number

Materials: None

About the Game

In most parts of the Canadian Arctic, winter means months without sunlight. During these days of darkness, Eskimos play games—many which involve sharp skills, concentration, and group cooperation. *Muk*, or Silence, is a game of mental concentration. The object is to remain in control and keep a straight face while another player tries to make you laugh.

Playing the Game

1. Choose one player to be IT. Have the other players form a circle around IT.

2. IT chooses a person to say the word "*muk*." This person must remain silent and in control—no laughing or twitching—while IT says funny things and makes strange faces to "break the *muk*."

Ending the Game

If the player breaks the *muk* he or she is given a funny name and is IT.

El Reloj

Skills: Jumping, timing, counting, coordination and rhythm skills

Ages: 6 and older

Players: 13

Materials: Jump rope or other rope approximately 18 feet (5.5 meters) long

About the Game

For thousands of years, adults and children have been jumping rope and using the skills needed to play this game—running, leaping, hopping—for survival. This game, *El Reloj* (pronounced reh-LOH) which means the clock, comes from the lower region of North America.

Playing the Game

1. Twelve players form a circle. They are the NUMBERS on the clock. A thirteenth player stands in the middle and holds the rope. This player acts as the clock's HAND.

2. On the count of 12, the middle player slowly begins to sweep the rope around the "clock." The NUMBERS jump over the rope as they shout out their numbers.

3. Each time the HAND makes a complete turn, it starts moving faster. Players who touch or stop the rope are out of the game.

Winning the Game

The last person left, wins.

Chapete

Skills: Balance, agility and fast reflexes

Ages: 9 and older

Players: 4 to 6

Materials: Outside playing area

Hacky Sack ball or hand-made ball a little smaller than your fist

About the Game

Where did *Hacky Sack* come from? California? Florida? Guess again. This centuries-old game originated in Mexico and is popular in Central and South America. *Chapete* has long been considered a game of quickness, super-sharp reflexes, and concentration.

To make a ball use a tough, pliable fabric as the case and fill it with dried beans, sand, or rice or a combination of the three.

Playing the Game

1. Players form a circle and stand not too far apart from each other. Play begins when the ball is tossed up and players take turns bouncing it off their body parts. Players are allowed to use any body part but their hands.

2. The object is to keep the ball from hitting the ground for as long as possible—while trying hard not to fall, crash into, or kick a team member.

Indian Kickball

Skills: Large motor skills and speed

Ages: 7 and older

Players: 3 to 6 players per team

Materials: 2 rubber balls about the size of baseballs (mark each ball with a different color)

Field markers: Chalk, paper plates, cloth, etc.

Stopwatch or watch with a second hand

Playing ground

About the Game

To the *Tarahumara* (ta-rau-MA-ra) Indians in northern Mexico, spring is more than the beginning of the growing season. Spring signals the start of kickball. A sport many children hope to be champions of.

This is no ordinary version of kickball. For starters, Tarahumara Indians only wear one shoe—usually a sandal—leaving their kicking feet bare (your students can leave their shoes on). Teams are small, between three to six players to a side. Each side has its own small ball which players kick back and forth and toss in the air using their toes. Finally, the playing field may be anywhere from 20- to 40-miles-long! It's easy to understand why the name Tarahumara comes from an Indian word meaning foot-runners.

Playing the Game

1. Name one end of the play area as the starting line and the other as the finish. Place five to 10 field markers between the start and finish line as obstacles for running around.

2. Divide the players into two teams. Teammates must work together to maneuver their ball as quickly as possible around the field markers to the other end of the field. Encourage your students to think about what real obstacles the Indians might run into over a 40-mile course.

Winning the Game

The first team to make it over the finish line wins.

Trier

Skills: Large and small motor skills, quickness and eye-hand coordination

Ages: 8 and older

Players: 2 or more

Materials: 5 pebbles or dried beans for each player

About the Game

Here's a game that takes extra-quick reflexes. Children in Trinidad play this anywhere they can find a few small pebbles. It's a popular game to play while waiting for a bus.

Playing the Game

1. Ask players to wiggle their fingers to limber up their hands.

2. Standing a short distance apart, have each player toss his or her beans up in the air with one hand and try to catch them all on the way down. Once players have mastered this, have them try the next step.

3. Now have players throw the beans up, but rather than catch them in their palms, catch them on the *backs* of their hands. Finally, with one smooth motion, tell them to flip the beans resting on the backs of their hands to their palms.

4. Players score points by how many beans they end up catching in their palms. So, if a player doesn't catch any—the score is zero.

Winning the Game

At the end of three rounds, the player with the highest score, wins.

All-tes-teg-enuk

Skills: Counting and probability

Ages: 7 and older

Players: 2

Materials: Plastic bowl or container

6 peach pits or similar shaped items

Paint (any color)

48 small sticks (approximately one inch or 2.5 centimeters long) or other small counters

5 larger sticks

About the Game

All-tes-teg-enuk, or The Bowl Game, was popular with the Passamaquoddy Indians of Maine. The women in the tribe played this game using "dice" made from materials like fruit pits, animal teeth, and nut shells. They often painted a different colorful design on one side of each playing piece. Score is kept by moving sticks or other small counters from hand to hand.

Playing the Game

1. Paint once side of each fruit pit.

2. Players sit across from each other. One player puts all the pits into the bowl and slams the bowl (face up) on table. If a pit jumps out of the bowl, the player's turn is over.

3. Scoring:

   • Four pits facing the same way up: Player wins 3 small sticks. Four pits up after two consecutive turns: Player wins 9 small sticks. Four pits up after three consecutive turns: Player wins 12 sticks.

   • Five pits facing the same way up: Player wins 12 small sticks or one large stick. Five pits up after two consecutive turns: Player wins 36 small sticks or 3 large sticks. Five pits up after three consecutive turns: player wins 16 small sticks from his or her opponent's pile.

4. If the opponent doesn't have enough sticks, the player lays out one stick for every three that are owed him or her. When the sticks are available the player is paid back.

Winning the Game

The first to take all of his or her opponent's sticks, wins.

Awithlaknannai

Skills: Thinking, calculating and estimating skills

Ages: 7 and older

Players: 2

Materials: Copy of game board (page 98)

12 game pieces for each player, should be two different colors

About the Game

Awithlaknannai comes from the Zuni Indians of New Mexico. This game developed from the same family of games as *Alquerque* (page 84). Zuni Indian children love playing this game. If a board wasn't available, they would draw the diamond-shaped diagram on the ground and play with whatever pieces they could find.

Playing the Game

1. Players begin by arranging their pieces on the board as shown by the black and white dots. One player should place his or her pieces on the black dots, the other player's pieces are placed on the white dots.

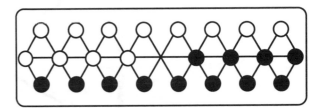

2. Toss a coin to decide who goes first. Players take turns moving their pieces to empty spots—jumping over and capturing an opponent's piece that's in the way of an empty space.

Winning the Game

The first to capture all of his or her opponent's pieces, wins.

Awithlaknannai
Game Board

Choosing Sides

Skills: Cooperation

Ages: All ages

Players: Chief (teacher) and a class of players

Materials: Two different colors or types of paper cut into strips (one strip per player)

Hat, shoe box, bag, something to hold the paper strips

Favorite book or other small object from each player

About the Game

Every culture has its own methods for choosing sides. For instance, in the United States, it's popular for children to "count off" to decide who will be on whose team. In many Native American cultures, practices for choosing sides were designed to avoid excluding or humiliating players who were picked last. Here are two simple ways for setting up teams that will help create team spirit. The Chief was usually the one put in charge.

Playing the Game

1. The CHIEF places an even number of strips of two different colors of paper in a sack. Holding the sack, the CHIEF asks players to come up one at a time, and pick a strip of paper without looking. Players who pull the same color strips form a team.

Variations of the Game

1. The CHIEF is in charge of this method as well. Ask each player to place a favorite book or small personal belonging in front of the CHIEF before forming a circle. (Native Americans piled their lacrosse sticks.)

2. The CHIEF is blindfolded and picks two objects at a time placing one in a pile on the left and one in a pile on the right until all the objects are distributed. Players then stand next to the pile with their objects and new team members.

Going to Boston

Skills: Counting and addition

Ages: 6 and older

Players: 2 or more

Materials: 3 dice

Paper

Pencil

About the Game

Here's a simple dice game that some believe began as a way to wile away the hours on the train to Boston. It's a simple game that can be played on any flat surface. Players can change rules as their skills develop. For example, this game can be played by adding, subtracting, or multiplying the numbers.

Playing the Game

1. Players roll a die to decide who goes first—low roll goes first.

2. Player one rolls all three dice and places the highest number to the side (only one side is saved, even if two three dice show the same number).

3. Now the player rolls two dice, and holds the highest one. Finally, only one die is rolled. The player adds up all three dice and writes the number down on paper.

4. Players repeat each step.

Winning the Game

The highest scorer after 5 rolls, wins.

Papago

Skills: Addition and guessing

Ages: 6 and older

Players: 2 or more

Materials: Four cups or cones

Marble or bean

Sand

About the Game

This game is popular with Native American children in the United States.

Playing the Game

1. Form teams using *Choosing Sides* on page 99, if there are more than two players.

2. One of the players conceals the marble in one of the four cups, fills them all with sand, and then gives the filled cups to his opponent or to the opposing team.

3. The opponent guesses which cup the marble is in. The fewer number of guesses it takes to discover the marble, the higher the score. Scoring is as follows:

Discovering marble on

• first try = 10 points

• second try = 6 points

• third try = 4 points

• fourth try = 0 points

Winning the Game

First player or team to score 50 points wins the game.

Sam Loyd's Game

Skills: Strategy and planning skills

Ages: 8 and older

Players: 1

Materials: Copy of game board (page 103)

Two types of beans or other counters—8 of each

About the Game

Since the 19th century, Sam Loyd has been considered a master inventor of tricks, puzzles, and games. This puzzle, which looks simple, really tests a player's thinking and planning skills.

Playing the Game

1. Place one type of bean (for example, we'll use red and white beans) in the boxes marked "red" and the other type in the boxes marked "white" (as shown in the diagram).

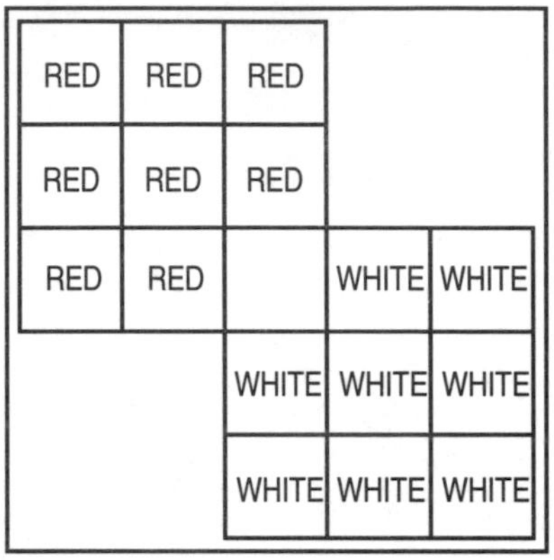

RED	RED	RED		
RED	RED	RED		
RED	RED		WHITE	WHITE
		WHITE	WHITE	WHITE
		WHITE	WHITE	WHITE

2. Rules for moving:

   • "Red" beans may only be moved to the right or down.

   • "White" beans may only move to the left and up.

   • Beans may move to an adjacent empty square, or may jump an adjacent bean with an empty space on the other side.

   • Beans may not make diagonal moves.

Winning the Game

Get the red beans where the white beans are, and the white beans where the red beans are in 46 moves or less.

Sam Loyd's Game Board

SOUTH AMERICA

Chicken Fight

Peteca

Hit the Penny

Shove Winter Out

Chicken Fight

Skills: Large muscle skills

Ages: 8 and older

Players: 2 or more

Materials: Handkerchief, scarf, or fabric piece for each player

Outdoor playing space

Chalk

About the Game

In many South American countries, chicken fighting is a popular sport where people place high bets on the outcome. Chickens used for fighting are specially bred. Children mimic the real thing through safe play.

Playing the Game

1. To begin the game, players draw one large circle (approximately 8 feet or 2.5 meters in diameter) on the ground.

2. Divide players into two teams (you may want to use one of the methods for Choosing Sides on page 99).

3. Two players enter the circle. Ask each player to tuck the scarf into his or her belt. Facing each other, players should act like chickens—making a wing with their right arms by folding them across their chests and hopping on one foot.

4. The object is for each player to try and grab the other's scarf without putting their feet down or unfolding their right arms.

5. The person who steps down first or un-folds an arm must leave the circle and surrender his or her scarf to the other team.

Winning the Game

Once everyone has had a turn, the team with the most scarves wins.

Peteca

Skills: Coordination and concentration

Ages: 9 and older

Players: 1 or more

Materials: Small bean bag or sock filled with sand

3 feathers

String

About the Game

This a popular party game in Brazil. It is played like the Mexican game of *Chapete* (page 93) but with a "ball" similar to the one used in the Asian game of *Shuttlecock* (page 50).

Playing the Game

1. Use the string to tie the feathers to the top of the bean bag or sock.

2. Players take turns tossing the bag up and hitting it with one hand back into the air as many times as they can without letting it touch the ground.

3. With each hit, the player says a letter of the alphabet or begins counting.

Winning the Game

The player to make it through the most letters without dropping or missing the bag, wins.

Variation of the Game

Have children try bouncing the bag off their knees or try reciting a poem as they play.

Hit the Penny

Skills: Coordination and aiming skills

Ages: 6 and older

Players: 4 and up

Materials: Broomstick or bamboo pole (12 to 18 inches or 30 to 45 centimeters long)

Penny for each player, plus one for the stick

Outside playing area (if playing indoors prop the stick up in a Christmas-tree stand)

About the Game

This game is popular with Chilean children and is often played outside. With the help of a Christmas-tree stand, the game can be played indoors. The game is a true test of aim.

Playing the Game

1. Bury one end of the stick in the ground so it stands up straight. Mark off a circle around the stick that is approximately 3 feet or 1 meter in diameter (the stick is in the center). Put the penny on top of the stick.

2. Have players stand about five feet from the stick. Taking turns, players try to knock the penny off the stick with their own penny.

3. A point is scored if the penny is knocked off the stick and out of the circle with a player's penny. No points are scored if the penny lands in the circle or isn't knocked off the stick.

Winning the Game

Player with the highest score wins.

Variation of the Game

Children may add to the game by marking off other circles within the one surrounding the stick and assigning these circles their own scores.

Shove Winter Out

Skills: Coordination and balancing skills

Ages: 6 and older

Players: 10 or more

Materials: Outdoor playing area or gym

Clothing tag or other identifiable marking for one group of team members

Watch with a second hand

About the Game

The people of the Tierra del Fuego Islands, off the southern tip of South America, battle winter for a large part of the year. Shoving winter out is a wish that many children living on the island have—that's how this game was created. The game may have a tendency to get a little rough, so it is usually played on soft, snow-covered ground. But a gym floor can work just as well, if players are careful.

Playing the Game

1. Divide the players into two teams. One team will be WINTER, the other SUMMER. One team should wear the tags (in Tierra del Fuego, children on the WINTER side mark their foreheads with coal).

2. Mark off a circular playing area, approximately 15 feet or 4.5 meters in diameter. The WINTER team stands around the inside of the circle, and the SUMMER team stands on the outside.

3. Both teams fold their arms across their chests—players must remain like this for the entire game. Anyone who drops his or her arms is out of the game.

4. During a set amount of time, the SUMMER team tries to shove the WINTER team out of the circle using only their backs and shoulders. WINTER team members who are shoved out become members of the SUMMER team.

5. When the time is up, players switch roles.

Bibliography

Barry, Sheila Ann, *Super Colossal Book of Puzzles, Tricks, and Games*, Sterling Publishing Company, New York, 1978.

Bell, R.C., *Board and Table Games from Many Civilizations*, Oxford University Press, 1969.

Bell, R.C., *Board and Table Games I,* Oxford University Press, London, 1960.

Brandreth, Gyles, *The World's Best Indoor Games*, Pantheon Books, New York, 1981.

Grunfeld, Frederi V., *Games of the World*, Holt, Rinehart and Winston, New York, 1975.

Harbin, E.O., *Games of Many Nations*, Abingdon Press, New York, 1954.

Hunt, Sarah Ethridge, *Games and Sports the World Around*, Third Edition, The Ronald Press Company, New York, 1964.

Murray, H.J.R., *A History of Board Games Other Than Chess*, Oxford at the Clarendon Press, 1952.

Orlick, Terry, *The Cooperative Sports and Games Book*, 1978.

Provenzo, Asterie Baker and Provenzo, Jr., Eugene F., *Favorite Board Games You Can Make and Play*, Dover Publications, Inc., New York, 1981.

Silverman, David L., *Your Move*, McGraw-Hill Book Company, New York, 1991.

Wiswell, Phil, *Kids' Games*, Doubleday and Company, Inc. New York, 1987.